EARLY AND MEDIEVAL CHRISTIAN SPIRITUALITY

Robert Imperato

University Press of America,® Inc.
Lanham · New York · Oxford

**Copyright © 2002 by
University Press of America,® Inc.**
4720 Boston Way
Lanham, Maryland 20706
UPA Acquisitions Department (301) 459-3366

PO Box 317
Oxford
OX2 9RU, UK

ISBN 0-7618-2430-8 (paperback : alk. ppr.)

Part I Major Authors

Part II Anthology

Introduction

This book intends to help make early and medieval Christian spiritual traditions accessible to the contemporary student by considering the major concerns of Christian spiritual teachings. This in turn may open new possibilities for spiritual development through contact with this tradition by exposing the reader to classical literature.

I am limiting discussion of the authors to the most fertile and influential in the tradition of Christian spirituality. I choose for example Cassian over Evagrius and other writers from the Egyptian desert because of Cassian's wide influence. Sometimes priority is the issue: The similarities between Clement and Origen are many; Clement's historical priority is a deciding factor. In other cases, depth and accessibility of texts in translation are factors in choosing among riches. These criteria of influence, priority, depth and accessibility I apply in a non-systematic way. I am confident that each of the people selected are significant, and know that there are others of towering genius that do not fit into this volume. Along with these considerations, I happen to like the writers chosen and trust that some will use this volume as an entry point into a treasure vault of Christian literature.

Spirituality refers to one's attitudes about life. As spiritual beings, we can coexist with ourselves, that is, I can observe and reflect upon my own thoughts and actions. I am spiritual in the sense that my awareness of the world and my awareness of my own thoughts do not take up two separate physical places. Generally, the language of spirituality occurs in religious contexts.

Religion is about relationship with ultimate and transcendent reality. Relationship suggests more than thought, and religion implies action as well as thought. I do not put the word God in this definition because of Buddhism, which does not see that talking about God is pertinent to the challenge of life. Buddhism is religion without God. Buddhism is how to deal with life, how to deal with suffering. Talking about God is a waste of time in Buddhism. Buddhists sometimes focus on transcendent experience, though not some sort of ecstasy. Buddhist transcendence involves transcending one's illusions. Transcendence in

Christianity includes that, but it also includes relating to a higher reality, namely God.

Spirituality focuses on attitudes, relationships; the transcendent part focuses on relations with ultimate reality and the practices that people associate with relating to God. It is possible to have spirituality without religion, for example human growth programs derived from 1960's human potential movement and humanistic psychology. Looking at one's attitudes and getting a handle on them is part of spirituality from all centuries. Religion and spirituality can exist apart or together.

Christian Spirituality refers to relationship with God and Christ, and the attitudes and practices associated with that relationship. How does this fit into a world religions perspective? Christian spirituality from a world religion point of view has these characteristics: it is a prophetic religion; it is often historically focussed, and it is personalistic. The prophetic traditions of Christianity, Judaism, and Islam are all religions of the word of God. Receptivity to that word and formation by the word of God are at the heart of these traditions. Christianity sees Jesus as God's manifestation, a word that God has interpreted for humans. Words of Jesus and words about Jesus are never far from view in Christian spirituality.

The words and deeds of Jesus become the prophetic utterances of God. Those words and deeds are ways to God. Jesus in the flesh is a manifestation and symbol of God, so the words of Jesus become representations of God.

What is a prophet? A prophet is one who has a keen insight into what God wants to communicate to a community. Prophets claim to be attuned to God's interiority. Prophets tend to say all say the same things; they speak of a need for repentance. Prophets say things people do not want to hear. Prophets say, "You people better get your acts together; you are not behaving properly. If you don't behave properly you are going to have trouble." Prophetic religion includes words from God, and these words are often a challenge to people's lives. Turn around; change! One of the major themes of Christian spirituality is repentance.

History is also an important consideration for Christianity. Hinduism and Buddhism do not care as much about history as they do in prophetic religion. Prophetic religions generally have a linear conception of time. The feast of unleavened bread illustrates the commitment of the biblical tradition to linear time and history.

The neighbors of Israel celebrated the first barley harvest each spring by making bread from the new harvest with no flour from the previous harvest. This celebration of newness of life occurred every year. Bread making involved taking some dough from the previous day and using it to leaven the new batch of dough. In the case of a celebration of a new harvest and the renewal of life implied, the bread dough could not benefit from the dough from the previous day with its yeast. That is why in this feast, the bread was unleavened. The feast of unleavened bread celebrated the recurring event of spring. Cyclical time focuses on recurring patterns.

Linear time, in contrast to cyclical time, highlights individual events in relation to each other. The biblically inspired religions thus focus on such individual events as the birth of Moses and the exodus from Egypt. These individual events become causes for celebration. When such a linear mentality encounters the cyclical understanding of the feast of unleavened bread, it transforms the meaning into something historical. Thus the biblical explanation for the feast of unleavened bread is haste! The Israelites escaped from the wrath of Pharaoh with such haste that there was not sufficient time for the dough to rise. (Exodus 12) Here the Biblical tradition has taken a recurring pattern from cyclical time in agriculture and endowed it with a historical once and for all setting. History in prophetic religions is this important. It is the arena for God's activity and for humans encountering God.

Christian remembrance of particular events is part of Christian consciousness. When Jews celebrate Passover, they remember. At the Passover meal, the people at table read from a book that contains stories of Jewish history, and one of the male children says, "Why are things different tonight with unleavened bread, bitter herbs, and the door unlocked?" The father will say, "When we were slaves in Egypt, we were liberated and we had to get out of town fast, we did not have time for our bread to rise. That is why we are eating unleavened bread: to commemorate our liberation from slavery in Egypt." Passover is about remembrance, and the remembrance has an impact because it refers to when "we" were slaves, even though the reference is made in the 21st century. By identifying with the Jews of the past, Jews in the present participate in the history of the Jewish experience of God. The history of the people in the past they appropriate, and this becomes a vehicle for their contemporary experience of God. They think that the God that liberated the Jews thousands of years ago will liberate them in their time of crisis. History is a link to experiencing God.

Christians use the ritual of Eucharist as a remembrance in the way Jews use Passover. Christians remember Jesus' death and resurrection in order to link with history and inform the future with the power of that history. Remembrance energizes people to step into the future with the power of God.

The personalism of early Christianity is rooted in the human person of Jesus as manifestation of God and in his relationship with his God. Christians are invited to share in that confidence which enables them to address the creator of heaven and earth as *Abba*. The message of Jesus about God's acceptance; the God who lets the rain fall and sun shine on the morally upright as well as upon sinners (Mt. 5), opens fearful hearts to God as loving parent. The intimacy and freedom of life in the presence of a gracious God who offers life as a gift, is a foundation for not only inner peace but also for sharing that love with other persons.

Sources

The sources for early and medieval Christian spirituality are abundant. The Bible could be one's only source as all writers that follow, lean on that book. Biblical sources are well known and later writers deserve to have their pages turned. Early Alexandrian writers bring philosophical breadth to biblical insights. The writers of the deserts of Egypt and Israel offer practical wisdom and interior depth. The incomparable Augustine introduces spiritual autobiography and theological complexity to Christian literature. This will be a selective survey, not at all comprehensive. The brightest lights that developed a contemplative dimension to Christian life will find center stage. The institutionalization of this type of Christianity falls at the feet of Benedict of Norcia. His rule's impact on western religion finds sublime expression in the twelfth century Cistercians. The high Middle Ages with its growing urban population draw Christian focus beyond the cloister through the development of spirituality that is both active and contemplative. The life witness of Francis of Assisi and the writing of Bonaventure amply represent this moment in Christian history. The literature of 14th century mysticism is less influential than the other authors of this volume, but its beauty merits a hearing.

1. Biblical Perspectives

The prophetic, personalistic, and historical perspectives, though inseparable in the Bible, can help us through the vast horizons of biblical literature. Hebrew understanding of God is rooted in God's call to the people we now call Jews. That call expressed God's mercy for this people. God took initiative to guide and protect this people despite their past behavior. God, according to the Bible, made them his own people. This personalistic foundation permeates biblical traditions. God has entered into relationship with a people and will remain faithful to this people throughout its journey.

The prophetic element involves the calling of the people back to their relationship with God when they have strayed. God remains faithful when the people do not. Fidelity to God implies morally upright behavior and compassion for others.

The context for this relationship is history. The Jews became aware of their special connection with God in their exodus from Egypt and God's manifestations to the wandering people repeatedly called them back to relationship with Him.

All of these elements carry over into the New Testament. New Testament writers portray Jesus' disciples as the new people of God; twelve tribes of Israel become twelve apostles. The people of Israel as God's son (Exodus 4:22) as falling into temptation during 40 years in the desert (Dt. 8) becomes the new son of God who resists temptation in the desert during 40 days. (Lk. 4) First John talks about that God's initiative in loving people as the basis for loving God. Mark's Gospel begins with Jesus uttering a prophetic call to repentance. God's choice is independent of human behavior. The themes of love and repentance derive from Hebrew Scripture and carry through all of Christian spirituality.

What is the connection between love and conversion? Love is not an object. It is an activity, not something exotic. If one is going to love, in the way God loves, then one will change one's behavior. God wants to give himself to creatures. God wants to give his kind of loving to creatures, love is not an object; it is an activity.

There are long published discussions of the meaning of love and the type of love appropriate to God. Perhaps the best is Josef Pieper's *About Love*. Pieper accepts the distinction between two Greek words *eros* and *agape*. Eros is desiring love. The desire for beauty, truth, and goodness in Plato is eros; this is love motivated by the beauty, truth, or goodness of the object loved. Agape, which is used by New Testament writers, expresses unselfish love. This is love that is motivated by the goodness of the subject. When Francis of Assisi embraces the leper, it is not the beauty of the leper that "turns on" Francis. Rather his love is an overflow of goodness for the leper. God, Christians believe, is not motivated by a hope for gain, but God loves out of an overflow of His own goodness. The eros and agape distinction is helpful, especially when these two loves are not opposed. A person's erotic or desiring love of God or of a human being can lead to more unselfish love. (Though helpful, the linguistic foundation of this distinction is not solid as the term agape can be used to describe loving a bribe or rape in the Greek translation of the Bible, which New Testament writers used.)[1]

Berakah is a form of Jewish prayer that involves a blessing that is rooted in historical remembrance. This threefold prayer involves firstly an acknowledgement of God's goodness: "Blessed are you o King of the universe! The second part is the reason for blessing which involves remembrance: "for your have saved us from slavery." Finally there is further blessing: "Blessed be God forever." This type of prayer in the hands of Christians becomes a remembrance of God's love manifested in Jesus, and this becomes central to Christian worship in the Eucharist. The blessing of God is the same but the historical remembrance changes from exodus from Egypt to Jesus' life, death, and resurrection.

History is not only important in Christianity, but the historical element of Jewish history carries into Christianity through the Incarnation. Christians see Jesus as the embodiment of God. The words and deeds of Jesus as historical manifestations of God become the objects of Christian prayer and worship.

The events of Jesus' life become symbols of spiritual possibility. Christ in the desert becomes a source of an entire lifestyle for the desert monks of third and subsequent centuries. The so-called "hidden years" when Jesus lived in Nazareth as part of a family prior to any prophetic ministry become symbolic of humble, dedicated work. The ordinariness of life is filled with meaning thanks to this backdrop of

Jesus' presumed ordinariness in Nazareth. Jesus as healer, as preacher, as teacher, as peacemaker, as prophetic challenger, as sufferer and as martyr are seeds from history (in a less than technical sense of history) that grow into the lives of Christians. History is foundational, and this is inflated with meaning by becoming symbols of human possibility.

To some degree whether one becomes a political activist, a medical missionary, or a cloistered nun depends on which elements of Jesus' life one chooses to make central in one's life.

The New Testament and the Cross

Although early Christian experience builds upon Jewish experience, Christianity goes its own way. The major symbol for Christian churches is the cross. Two New Testament works that make the cross central are Mark's Gospel and Paul's first Letter to the Corinthians. These two works will help to explain implications for the cross for Christian life and also to show how the cross has become central.

The Cross and Mark's Gospel: Self-denial.

Love and conversion are persistent themes of Christian spirituality. If one reads the history of this tradition one will encounter heroic efforts of people willing to die for their faith, of people willing to starve themselves in order to master themselves, and of people willing to work tirelessly for others. How does Christianity generate heroic behavior? Its most effective source of breaking with convention is the cross of Jesus. This is a religion that holds up a dead man on a cross and suggests that following Jesus may mean sharing in what the cross symbolizes. Amazingly, such an unappetizing symbol has attracted countless numbers of people.

Mark's gospel offers the cross as the key to understanding who Jesus is and what discipleship entails. Mark accomplishes this focus on the cross and discipleship by establishing a pattern of recognition and lack of recognition. Jesus offers works of healing and exorcism, miraculous multiplication of loaves, challenge to the religious observances of his day, even walking on water, transfiguration and leaving his tomb after death! This spectacular resume of activities generates confusion and lack of recognition by his followers and by his witnesses. The only recognition of Jesus as Son of God comes from the demons and God and one human being. That human being was not Peter though Peter calls Jesus "Christ." Christ meant messiah or the anointed one who was going to take over the government thereby establishing God's rule. Jesus then tells Peter that Jesus will die soon in Jerusalem. Peter rebukes Jesus and in turn Jesus reprimands Peter. Mark portrays Peter as expecting a political takeover; instead he hears about Jesus' impending death; Jesus' death is incongruous for someone regarded to be the next head of government. Peter's misunderstanding becomes part of a pattern in chapters 8, 9, and 10 of Mark's Gospel.

Mark's Gospel Chapters 8, 9 and 10

These chapters primarily deal with instruction to the disciples and their lack of understanding. In each of the three chapters (8, 9, 10) there are four structural elements that help to organize the material:

Geographic Reference (GR) = Where instruction took place.

Passion Prediction (PP) = Where Jesus predicted His death.

Misunderstanding (M) = The disciples' misunderstanding which gives opportunity to explain discipleship.

Teaching on Discipleship (D) = Self-denial and service.

Chapter 8

(GR)   8:27 Caesarea Philippi.

(PP)   8:31 Jesus told the disciples that he must suffer many things and be rejected by elders, chief priests and scribes then be killed and rise again in three days.

(M)   8:32 Peter did not accept Jesus' death as he (Peter) still saw Jesus as the earthly messiah. As chapter 10 shows (10:35+) the other disciples anticipated Jesus' acquisition of governmental power. How can Jesus die if he is about to take over the rule of the government!

(D)   8:34-38 Jesus expounded on the role of the cross and pointed out that the worldly life is not profitable when one's soul is at stake. Whoever is ashamed of Him in the face of the world so will He be of them before God.

Chapter 9

(GR)   9:30 Galilee and Capernaum.

(PP)   9:31 And the Son of man is delivered into the hands of men and they shall kill him; and after he is killed, he shall rise the third day.

(M)   9:32 But they understood not that saying, and were afraid to ask him.

(D)   9:35-50 Here Jesus explains that the role of a servant is the way of discipleship.

          Chapter 10

(GR)   10:32 Jerusalem.

(PP)   10:33-34 Again, Jesus tells his disciples of his rejection death at the hands of the Jewish authorities and his resurrection in three days.

(M)   10:35-41 Two of the disciples asked to sit with him in glory (rule with him). When he asked if they were ready to drink his cup (to accept the same life as his) they answered affirmatively and he said they would have a similar life, but as to sitting beside him, that was up to God; it was not his (Jesus) to give.   This made the others angry, as they did not understand. Also the disciples still had not grasped his true meaning.

(D)   10:42-45 Jesus points out that in the world those which have authority exercise their authority, but among them (the disciples) the exercising of authority is not important. Paramount is ministering to others.

Mark repeats passion predictions three times in a row, and each is followed by misunderstanding. Mark repeats himself as if to warn the reader with a blinking neon sign, "Don't miss it." The disciples miss out on Jesus' identity, and Mark is warning the reader that it is easy to misunderstand what Jesus is saying and who he is.

The misunderstanding of chapters 8, 9, and 10 is part of the ongoing misunderstanding by the disciples and of the recognition of Jesus as Son of God by the demons, God, and one human being. That human being is the centurion at the foot of the cross (15:39) who is portrayed as seeing only Jesus dying. "When the centurion, who stood facing him, saw that he thus breathed his last, he said, 'Truly this man was son of God'" Recognition comes through seeing Jesus on the cross. Recognition is difficult because the cross is a symbol of discipleship.

After each misunderstanding in chapters 8, 9, and 10 the disciples are told to deny themselves, take up their cross, to be servant of all, to be last of all. These injunctions go against the grain of ordinary human aspiration.   To hear something that no one wants to hear is the difficulty of receptivity about which Mark is trying to caution the reader by repeating the passion predictions, the misunderstandings, and the teaching on discipleship.

The great works of power throughout this gospel, namely healing, casting out demons, and spectacular miracles do not generate understanding of Jesus as Son of God. The cross is the key.

The Cross in Paul's First Letter to the Corinthians

Another early use of the cross, earlier than Mark's Gospel is Paul especially in his First Letter to the Corinthians. Paul begins this letter in the first four chapters by reprimanding the Corinthians for the divisions within the community. People are inflating their egos by identifying with particular spiritual teachers: "I belong to Paul, I belong to Cephas, I belong to Apollos; I belong to Christ." Paul strives to convince these Corinthians that Christian life is not a matter of improving one's status by association with particular spiritual guides. The Corinthians have sought wisdom, strength, and honor, but Paul wants them to imitate himself and Christ crucified who was willing to appear foolish, weak, and dishonored on the cross. (See 1 Cor. 1:23-31; 4:6-13) This example of Christ crucified becomes the basis for solving numerous problems in Corinth.

In addition to bringing unity to the community, the cross becomes a symbol of the principle of self-sacrifice for the sake of the community. In chapter 6, the question of whether Christians ought to sue one another, Paul answers with the cross: Why not suffer wrong? Why not rather be defrauded? (1. Cor. 6:7) This is consistent with non-retaliation by Jesus against his persecutors, thus the Corinthians should respond in kind. What this avoidance of lawsuits can do is maintain the unity of the community.

In chapters eight and ten, the question of whether Christians should eat meat that has been sacrificed to idols leads Paul to acknowledge that Christians are free to eat any type of food, and there are no other gods. He cautions, however, that not all Christians are clear about these matters and might become confused by seeing disciples of Jesus eating such meat. For the sake of the less than enlightened Paul suggests that people refrain from eating such food. Thus for the sake of the community, do not eat meat sacrificed to idols. He gives in chapter nine the example of himself who has the right to be paid for being an apostle, but for the sake of the community he refrains from exercising his right. This is also the principle he applies to celebration of the Eucharist in chapter 11; celebrate in a way that will not humiliate the poor. In this case Paul asks the Corinthians to alter the way they celebrate the Eucharist by eliminating the real meal to which the poor would have nothing to contribute, and keep the ritual partaking of bread and wine. Self-sacrifice for the community is also his guiding principle in the question of spiritual gifts and speaking in tongues in chapters 12-14.

Speaking in tongues is good, but the better gifts are those that serve others not just oneself. Chapter 13 is a description of what Paul means by love: " Love does not insist on its own way."

Paul like Mark uses the cross as a symbol of self-denial for the sake of following Jesus, for the sake of service, and for the sake of the community.

The cross as symbol of self-denial and self-sacrifice sets the tone for Christian experience in all subsequent centuries. The backdrop of such self gift is acceptance of God's love as expressed in the compassionate ministry of Jesus (touching outcasts), in Jesus' prayer to God as Abba, and in Jesus' assertion that God's love is for the just and the unjust (Mt. 5:45). Without the experience of being loved and accepted by God, efforts at self-sacrifice will likely include an inner tyranny that is void of peace. In the security of being loved unconditionally, Christians attempt to echo that love in their service of the community.

If one looks at Jesus as a reformer of Judaism, he was trying to challenge the way people were relating to God and one another. One of the basic things he was teaching was about Abba. Jesus' addressed God with the familiar term for God; Jewish writings do not use Abba as an address for God for many centuries after Jesus. That kind of familiarity with God says something about who God is for Jesus.

I relate Abba to a Greek word in Acts of Apostles characteristic of disciples of Jesus: *parrhesia,* meaning free speech and filial confidence. How does free speech relate to filial confidence? I remember sitting in my father's lap and playfully poking him in the stomach. It was clear to me that there was nothing I could do to move him to turn his love for me away. The playful freedom to do and say what I wished is freedom of speech and filial confidence. This is what disciples of Jesus may have according to the New Testament (See Acts 4: 29, 31; 1 Jn.2: 28, 3:21, 4:17, 5:14).

Freedom to be oneself is a function of being accepted and loved. If I am accepted, I need not always try to prove myself. That kind of freedom, I associate with the kind of freedom that Jesus had in relation to God: freedom to speak, to be intimate, informal, to be oneself.

Clash with Culture

Early Christianity was not a complete break with culture. Jesus attempted to reform Judaism, and Paul found that Christian understanding could endure life without bondage to Jewish law. Jesus challenged some of the priorities related to Sabbath (Mk. 2) and introduced Abba as a way of relating to God. Jesus' reforms were sufficiently challenging to the status quo that his opponents thought it expedient to kill him. At the same time Jesus went to the Temple and had respect for Jewish scripture; he was not out to destroy Judaism.

Paul declared his religious education to be refuse (Philippians 3) and saw dependence on God rather than on one's ability to observe religious regulations as the key to life. (Galatians and Romans) Paul did his best to challenge religious faith if it insulated one from God rather than opened one to God. If a person thought that keeping all of the rules and regulations of religion took care of God, or handled God, then Paul comes in with a scalpel to peal away false security in one's ability. This surgery he designed to expose dependence on the gracious God who offers life as a gift. Paul used Jewish tradition but dramatically transformed it so that gentiles could relate to God with the same liberty as any Jew.

The Jesus traditions as well as Paul indicate transformation of tradition but not a compete break with the past. The same transformation occurs with regard to Hellenism.

Hellenism

If I am a Greek living somewhere in Asia Minor and I begin believing in the God of Paul, I am going to break somewhat from my culture. There are educated Christians who attempted to include elements of Hellenistic culture into their Christian understanding. A few words about martyrdom will serve as a transition to Hellenism.

Paul's break with his Jewish past, though incomplete (he continued to ponder God's plan for the Jews in Romans 9-11) was world shaking for himself and gives expression to the heroism of early Christianity. "But whatever gain I had [as a Jew], I counted as loss for the sake of Christ."(Phil. 3) This heroism of total commitment found expression in his willingness to die ("My desire is to depart and be with Christ" Phil. 1:23) and in later willingness to die for one's faith in the early Christian martyrs. When the early bishop, Ignatius of Antioch desired to be eaten by the lions in Rome, he was not escaping from life so much as desiring to be with Christ in heaven.

As Christianity became more accepted by the Roman Empire, martyrdom diminished in its popularity. The early Jewish persecution of Christians subsided and Romans were only intermittently hostile. When persecutions subsided martyrdom gave way to what Clement of Alexandria called "gnostic martyrdom."

> If martyrdom consists in confessing god, every person who conducts himself with purity in the knowledge of God, who obeys the commandments, is a martyr in his life and in his words: in whatever way his soul is separated from the body, he will pour out his faith in the manner of blood, all during his life and at the moment of his exodus. This is what the Lord says in the Gospel: 'Whoever leaves his father, his mother, his brothers, etc. because of the Gospel and my name,' such a man is blessed because he realizes not only ordinary martyrdom but the Gnostic martyrdom, in living and acting according to the rule of the Gospel, by love for the Lord. For gnosis is the knowledge of the Name and the understanding of the Gospel. (Clement of Alexandria, *Stromata* 4. 4. 15 quoted by L. Bouyer in his *The Spirituality of the New Testament and the Fathers* (N.Y.: Seabury Press, 1963), p.210)

A few broad strokes on the difference between Hebraic (biblical) culture and Hellenistic culture will help set the stage for Clement of Alexandria's thought.

Hellenistic is more human centered than Hebraic. Sin in Hebraic culture is disobedience to God or offensive against God. In, Hellenistic culture, sin is being unfaithful to one's self. God in Hebraic culture is caring and compassionate. The Hebrew God feels; he gets angry and is happy. This God gets angry with people of Israel when they are wandering through the desert, and they don't trust in him.

In Hellenistic culture God is passionless. Passion has to do with emotions. The opposite of passion is action according to Aristotle. This is why some Greek writers would not want God to have passion. Passion for Greeks sometimes suggests weakness. If one is pushed around by anger or any other emotion, one is passive to it and weaker than such emotions. To suggest God is weak would have been unacceptable to some strands of Greek thought, hence God is passionless. The human ideal associated with this type of a God is someone who is above the influence of passion. This is someone who makes judgment according to what is right and is cool and reasonable in all situations. The human ideal in the Hebraic tradition is the prophet, who is attuned in to God's feeling.[2] The meeting of these two traditions in the period in which Christianity is born leads some Christian writers to reinterpret Hebraic understandings into Greek.

A prominent Jew who attempted to transform biblical understandings into those more acceptable to Greeks was Philo of Alexandria, a contemporary of Paul. Philo illustrates the Hellenization of biblical material in his short treatise *The Unchangeableness of God.* The God of the Torah expresses emotion, hence change, and from a Greek point of view, weakness. Philo quotes God from Genesis: "I will blot out man who I made from the face of the earth." (Gen. 6:7) Philo continues:

> Some on hearing these words suppose that the Existent feels wrath and anger, whereas He is not susceptible to any passion at all. For disquiet is peculiar to human weakness, but neither the unreasoning passions of the soul, nor the parts and members of the body in general, have any relation to God. All the same the Lawgiver uses such expressions, just so far as they serve for a kind of elementary lesson, to admonish those who could not otherwise be brought to their senses. (*Unchangeableness of God* 11. 52)

This contrast between Greek and Hebraic understanding helps to open up the thought of Clement of Alexandria.

2. Clement of Alexandria (ca.150-215 c.e.): Reason, Virtue, Image of God

Little is known about the life of Clement of Alexandria; he lived in the latter half of the second century, and various modern sources date his death at 215 or 230 c.e.

Clement could easily be grouped with Christian Platonists, but because of his relative priority among the Hellenistically formed Christian writers I locate him here as an example of one who consciously expands Christian thought into Hellenistic terms. His Platonism is no less noticeable than later writers, but I postpone discussion of Platonism after this general introduction to Hellenized Christianity.

In Christianity, a favorite expression for relationship with God is to be an image and likeness of God. This notion of image, central to Christian anthropology and spirituality, principally derives from Greek and Hebraic sources. The principal biblical source is Genesis 1:26, where God creates humans in His image and likeness by giving them dominion over all other creatures. Plato supplies the Greek notion of image by conceiving of earthly reality as imaging a higher realm upon which the understanding person will pattern life. "The city whose home is in the ideal . . .perhaps there is a pattern of it laid up in heaven for him who wishes to contemplate it and so beholding to constitute himself its citizen." (From *Republic* 592; see also *Timaeus* 29 and *Theatetus* 176 b.) The New Testament speaks of Christ as the image of God (Rm. 8: 29, Heb. 1:3; 1 Jn. 3:2; Col. 1:15; 2 Cor. 4:4), thus fostering Patristic discussions of image.

Clement and Non-Christian Sources

Clement's teaching on image and likeness resembles an earth dwelling inconspicuously built in the side of a hill rather than a skyscraper sitting upon concrete with no relationship to the surrounding land. Clement's Christianity builds in harmony with culture. Clement (in agreement with Philo and Justin Martyr) believes that Greek philosophers can know God and truth because all people are gifted with reason. He acknowledges that Platonists and Pythagoreans agree with the Bible that reason is God's gift (*Stromata* 5. 87-88) Clement further sees the mind (*nous*) as an image or imitation of God's own image, the Logos (*Stromata*.5. 94). Before the coming of Christ, God guided the Greeks through philosophy and gave preparatory formation by increasing faith through demonstration (*Stromata*.1. 28). Clement ascribes prophetic inspiration to Pythagoras and Plato (*Stromata*. 5. 29; 7. 6).

However much Clement appreciates truth in Greek philosophy, he maintains the pre-eminence of Biblical and Christian revelation. He believed, for example, that Plato was taught by the Hebrews themselves. (*Exhortation to the Greeks* 6). Clement's openness to Greek philosophy allows Christianity to benefit from philosophy, and his belief that Greeks took ideas from the Hebrews defends his religion from the attacks of those Hellenists, such as Celsus, who interpret Christianity as an imitation of Greek philosophy.[3]

Inasmuch as biblical and Christian revelation is normative for Clement, he is critical toward various philosophies. He praises Plato and Pythagoras as being in harmony with Moses' teaching. (*Stromata* 5. 29) He respects Plato because he recognizes the goal of human life is to be likeness to God. (*Stromata* 2. 100). Other philosophers do not fare as well under Clement's gaze. He condemns Epicureans who eliminate Divine Providence and divinize pleasure (*Stromata* 1.50) and accuses Aristotle of the same (1. 90) Clement says that the Stoics juggle logic by teaching that God is material. (1. 51) In short Clement sees God communicating truth to all through reason and prophecy, and people may be guided by those philosophers that are in harmony with Christian teaching.

Clement on Image and Likeness

As noted above the (1) Image of God for Clement is the God-given reflection in human beings of the Logos. The (2) Likeness refers to human perfection achieved by effort with God's help. Attainment of likeness to God is through a (3) life of virtue. Such (4) progress moves from moderation of the passions to (5) *apatheia* when one is freed from domination by passion by the (6) guidance of the Divine Teacher,

Christ, toward likeness to God. The (7) individual virtues that Clement discusses give a picture of his understanding of Christian life, a picture somewhat more active than the speculative life often associated with Alexandrian Christianity.

Image of God

The Image of God for Clement is Christ, the Logos. Christ fulfills the divine decree "Let us make man in our image and likeness." (Gen.1: 26) Human beings are images of the perfect Image. Clement plays on the dual meaning of logos: reason and Word of God.

> Heraclitis said well 'men are gods and gods are men, for reason is the same' (Fragment 62)—manifestly a mystery. God is in man and a man is God, as the Mediator, fulfilling the will of His Father. For the reason common to both is the mediator; that is, the Word, Son of God, savior of man, the servant of God, our Educator. (*Instructor* 3. 2)

All humans image the Image since all have reason. Clement follows Plato's *Republic* that describes the human soul in three parts: (1) the intelligence, (2) anger, and (3) desire. The intelligence or reason "is the inner man, the ruler of the external man. But it is led by someone else, that is by God." (*Instructor* 3. 2) The reason or intelligence Clement identifies with "breath of life" breathed into matter when God made Adam. (*Stromata*.5. 87-88)

Likeness to God

The likeness is not a static endowment of human nature but rather a perfection, an achievement, a realization, a goal. Clement uses Plato's likeness ("Evils. . .can never be done away with, for the good must always have its contrary: nor have they any place in the divine world, but they must needs haunt the region of our mortal nature. That is why we should make all speed to take flight from this world to the other, and that means becoming like the divine so far as we can, and that again is to become righteous with the help of wisdom." *Theatetus* 176b) to God in interpreting the Christian teaching on image and likeness. (*Stromata* 2. 131) The likeness to God, to the Image Christ is achieved by following Christ the Teacher, and Clement thematizes this following as becoming like God in terms of virtues.

> We are educated not for war but for peace. In war there is need for much equipment, just as self-indulgence craves an abundance. But peace and love, simple and plain blood sisters do not need arms nor abundant supplies. Their nourishment is the Word, the Word whose leadership enlightens and educates, from whom we learn poverty and humility and all that goes with love of freedom and of mankind and of the good. In a word through Him we become like God by a likeness of virtue. (*Instructor* 1. 12)

Life of Virtue

The life of virtue for Clement highlights his recognition that Christian life is not restricted to interiority but involves a person's entire life. "Virtue is a disposition of soul attuned (*symphonos*) to the dictate of reason in the whole course of life."(*Instructor* 1. 13) Clement acknowledges the source for his description of virtue as the Stoics who speak of virtuous action in terms of obedience to reason. Clement applies this idea of virtue to a more biblical idea where obedience begins or is founded upon commands. (1. 13) He often speaks of gnosis, but the life of virtue is clearly dependent upon the will: "he who would have virtue must choose it."(*Stromata* 7. 9) Virtuous action includes the dutiful, and a human being's duty is "to cultivate a will that is in conformity and united throughout his life to God."(*Instructor* 1. 102) A life according to reason is a life in conformity to God. Reason carries the dual meaning of rationality and the Word of God:

> The life of a Christian . . . is a united whole made up of deeds controlled by reason; that is, it is the persevering accomplishment of the truths taught by reason, or rather, the Word, an accomplishment which we call fidelity. (*Instructor* 1. 102)

The omnipresence of the Word of God enables Clement to affirm so simply the congruence of reason and the Word. The word communicates through the teachings of Christ, the biblical tradition, and through reason. As virtue grows so does likeness to God, though likeness is not identify with God. (*Stromata* 7. 88)

Progress

Clement's spirituality of image and likeness is one of progress in virtue. The ethical problem, which Clement discusses, is that humans are not as free as they should be on account of the domination of the passions. The moderation of passion Clement sees as preparatory to eradication of passion. For example, fear of the Lord diminishes malice and the power of fear; this diminishment leads toward mastery of passions though not passionlessness. (2. 39) Elsewhere Clement writes similarly of moderating desires to natural proportions (7. 109) and of "the middle course" as "good in all things." (*Instructor* 2) Such moderation is part of the road to recovery from the disease of the passions: "reason is the ruling principle of the passions of the soul, which we master by means of virtue: it impresses self-control, temperance and piety (upon the soul). (*Instructor,* 1. 154). Clement sees passions as a disease because they are impulses that go beyond the measure of reason. Passions involve disobedience to reason. (*Stromata* 2. 59)

This disobedience Clement calls sin: "everything contrary to right reason is a sin."(*Instructor* 1, 13) Passion is against reason and thus lowers the rational animal to the level of the irrational. Such a one becomes a dumb animal without words or reason, directed by "every sort of pleasure."(1. 13). Progress in virtue implies progress in self mastery particularly with reference to the passions, but Clement would have the Christian go beyond moderation to passionlessness.

Apatheia

Clement frequently refers to passionlessness or apatheia in describing the perfect Christian, the gnostic. (Clement's type of gnosticism is orthodox, not the same type of heterodox gnosticism usually associated with this period in history.) The passage from faith (*pistis*) to knowledge (*gnosis*) is another way Clement has of describing spiritual progress. Pistis involves a fairly superficial relationship with the mysteries of Christianity, a belief in the Scriptures without a deeper penetration: "while they who have but tasted of the Scriptures are believers, the gnostics, who have made further progress, are accurate judges of the truth; since even in the ordinary concerns of life craftsmen have an advantage over laymen."(*Stromata* 7. 95) The gnostic discerns the truth of Christian teaching, and love gives the gnostic access to deeper understanding. "Since the truth does not belong to everybody, it is kept hidden in several ways: it illuminates only those people who are initiated into gnosis, namely those who, being moved by love, search after it."(*Stromata* 6. 129) The gnostic is purified and can thus rest in and contemplate (*theorias*) God. (See *Stromata*. 7. 7. 61 and 7. 83). In order to enter into contemplation one must achieve apatheia that involves, in part, detachment from sensible and earthly things.

> We raise the head and lift the hands toward heaven, and stand on tip toe as we join in the closing outburst of prayer, following the eager flight of the spirit into the intelligible world; and while we thus endeavor to detach the body from the earth by lifting it upwards along with the uttered words, we spurn the fetters of the flesh and constrain the soul, winged with desire of better things to ascent into the holy place. (*Stromata* 7. 40)

The detachment from the sensible in order to enter into communion with the intelligible Clement sees as necessary because material things are always attracting desire and "desire. . .seeks. . . to conceal the true nature of a human being." If one is running after external objects one is likely to fail to be directed by reason. "Reason is the inner human" and should be "the ruler of the external human," and should be led by God. The pull of sensible objects on human motivation is strong enough to interfere with one's orientation toward God. The person who is not tossed about by passion may be guided by reason, hence is like God. (*Instructor* 3. 1)   The gnostic who has tamed response to bodily pleasures and pains is "in accordance with the divine likeness."(*Stomata* 7. 3) In Clement's view, Christ, the perfect Image, attained mastery of his passions (7. 2); the Divine Reality is without passion. (2. 72; 2. 81) The gnostic possesses interior resources and thus is not dependent on the opinions of others. (7.3) In a word the gnostic is free because the gnostic is tuned to the Divine Will.

The emphasis on attainment and self sufficiency in Clement should not obscure the most profoundly Christian dimension of apatheia, namely that which is born of love.

> If the gnostic does not have desire, some people say, he can no longer eagerly strive towards the resembling of perfect men. If, then, all intimacy with the good is realized in virtue of a tendency, how then, they say, can he who tends towards the good remain 'apathetic'? But these men do not understand, it seems the divine character of love. For love is no longer a tendency of him who loves: it is a loving intimacy, which establishes the gnostic in the unity of faith, without his having any further need of time nor of space. Already established by love in the good things that he will possess, having anticipated hope by gnosis,

he no longer tends towards anything, having everything that he could tend towards. He remains, then, in the one unchanging attitude, loving in gnostic fashion, and he does not have to desire to be made like beauty, for he possesses beauty by love. What need is there now of courage or of desire for this man who has gained loving intimacy with the God who is passionless and who is himself inscribed among his friends by love? For us, the perfect gnostic must be removed from any passion of the soul. (*Stromata* 6. 9 quoted by Bouyer, pp. 273-274.)

Thus apatheia is a deep contentment born of love. The one who is in communion with the Beloved does not have to attempt to climb the mountain of the Lord with desperation. The one who has this kind of an arrival experience, however fleeting, knows that the love of God is holding all in being. Likeness to God thus issues from knowledge of His love. (See also *Instructor* 1. 3) Clement affirms the ascetical effort helpful in freeing a person from the domination of passion, but the power of Divine love has the greatest transforming effect.

Personal Help of the Divine Teacher

The focus on God's love and the power of that love to effect change is a particularly Christian element in Clement which is not to be found in his non-Christian sources. The meaning of logos in Clement would help at this point. Lilla summarizes three meanings of the Logos for Clement: (1) The Logos is the mind of God containing the thoughts of God. (*Stromata* 4. 15) (2) The Logos is the immanent law of all things inasmuch as the ideas are the patterns for all things. (5. 38) (3) The Logos is also God's adviser. To these I would add (4) Logos as Sacred Scripture (*Instructor* 1. 103) Since all of these understandings of Logos may be found in Philo,[4] one may ask whether anything uniquely Christian may be found in Clement's presentation of Logos.

What Lilla finds in Clement and not in any of his non-Christian sources is the personal way the logos intervenes in human life and transformation. The Logos "lovingly guides"(*Instructor* 1. 3) Christians. Into seekers God "breathes . . . strength for the completion of their salvation."(*Stromata*.2. 48) The Logos is the Educator: "The Word . . . teaches all things and use all things to educate us . . . man is reformed by the Word by whom He tamed as though he were a wild beast." (*Instructor* 3. 99) The metaphor of the intervention of the Word as taming a beast is strong, but coercion is not the way Clement understands the manner in which Christ works. Christ the Teacher educates, applies corrective discipline, and persuades. (*Stromata* 7. 6) Although Clement emphasizes the necessity of living according to reason, he sees such living as a cooperation between the Christian and the Logos: "reason translated into deeds under the guidance of the educator."(*Instructor* 3. 35) Through the guidance of the Logos a human being is reshaped into the likeness of God.

The specific virtues in this project of imaging God according to Clement will clarify his vision of Christian life. As we have seen Clement believes that the life of virtue is the way to image God. Virtue involves living according to reason and according to Christ. Attainment of freedom from the passions is an ascetical goal as well as a fruit of knowing Christ.

Clement notes interior virtues when discussing the likeness to Christ, but more generally he relates imaging Christ to action. Of the interior virtues steadfastness and self-sufficiency stem from being grounded in truth. A Christian so dependent on the Logos will not be dependent on external sources for happiness; such a dedicated Christian will be trusting in God sufficiently to be living in the present moment without anxiety for tomorrow. (*Instructor* 1. 98) This interior freedom comes from knowledge of Christ. (*Stromata* 7. 86) One who is becoming like Christ will manifest devoutness (7. 3), but true to the new commandment Clement focuses on attitudes and actions related to other people when discussing likeness.

The perfect gnostic will manifest conformity to Christ through action. (*Instructor* 1. 99; 3. 35) To be assimilated to God one must become free from passion because God is free from passion, but this development of freedom is not in isolation from other people. The work of the perfect gnostic is to hold communion with God through service:

> . . . being made like the Lord, as far as may be by means of service towards God a service which extends to the salvation of men by his solicitous goodness . . . by public worship and by teaching and active kindness . . . and in being thus assimilated to God, the gnostic is making and fashioning himself and also forming those who hear him. (*Stromata* 7. 3)

In service to others one is transformed into the likeness of the perfect Image. The gentleness and kindness of Christ becomes actualized in attending to the salvation of others. The religious education of others becomes one's way to assimilation to God.

The three achievements of the gnostic consist " (1) in the knowledge of the facts of the Christian religion, (2) in the accomplishment of whatever the word enjoins, (3) in the capacity to impart to others after a godly manner the hidden things of truth."(7. 4) The religious educator is more than one who gives information. The true gnostic is a mediator of fellowship with God and affects the character of others by doing good and regards "good done to his neighbor as his own salvation." Thus the gnostic becomes "a living image of the Lord." (7. 9)

In addition to Clement holding up religious education as a fine context for imaging God, his most striking commitment to active love is in his appreciation of marriage.

> True manhood is shown not in the choice of a celibate life: on the contrary the prize in the contest of men is won by him who has trained himself by the discharge of the duties of husband and father and by the supervision of a household, regardless of pleasure and pain, --by him, I say, who in the midst of his solicitude for his family shows himself inseparable from the love of God and rises superior to every temptation which assails him through children and wife and servants and possessions. On the other hand he who has no family is in most respects untried. In any case, as he takes thought only for himself, he is inferior to one who falls short of him as regards his own salvation but who has the advantage in the conduct of life, as much as he actually preserves a faint image of the true Providence. (*Stromata* 7. 70)

This long quotation demonstrates the willingness of Clement to advocate self-sacrificial love. The passage makes the ascetical point that one who is in solitude will not be tried as one in marriage, but more pertinent to the theme of image is the comment that by having to care for others a person will be more forgetful of self and will image Divine Providence.

Clement, true to the New Testament, affirms that one advances in Christian life through love (*Stromata* 7. 84), and this love implies forgiveness. He gives several reasons for not retaliating against one who is hostile. Firstly, one who attempts to inflict harm can only harm the external, and the gnostic would be above such concerns. Secondly, judging the actions of another would lead one to become "an apostate from the Gospel." Finally, seeking retaliation against someone fails to see the possibility of those others coming to believe in Christ. This last reason touches the issue of imaging because the person with true Christian understanding will recognize, ". . .that all men are the work of one God, invested with one image upon one nature." Thus imaging God includes awareness that all are loved by God, that all are His images. This awareness serves love as the awareness of the depth of another image inspires love, longsuffering, and forgiveness. (7. 84-87) This final insight in the discernment of the image in others connects gnosis and apatheia and whatever attention Clement gives to consciousness with active charity.

3. Platonism: Plato (ca. 428-348 b.c.e.) and Plotinus (ca. 205-270 c.e.): Symbols of Transformation:

The example of Clement illustrates the influence of Hellenism and of Greek philosophy on a Christian spiritual writer as well as the openness among some Christians to Greek philosophy. The Platonic tradition is the most powerful philosophical influence on Christian thought until the thirteenth century when Aristotelian influence comes into the West. Platonism gives Christian thinkers a set of universal symbols that in turn gives both vocabulary and imagery to aid Christians in conceptualizing elements of spiritual life. These universal symbols become part of standard Christian teaching for all subsequent generations. A brief exposure to Plato and to Plotinus as a key Platonist will highlight these symbols. I will illustrate the use of these symbols by such later Christian writers as Augustine, Gregory of Nyssa, and Dionysius the Areopagite. There is no suggestion that Gregory of Nyssa derived his Platonism from Plotinus though both he and Augustine most likely read Plotinus, rather that Plotinus is as influential as any Platonist on all Christians who followed him.[5]

Some of the symbols that Christians derived from Platonists overlap with Biblical symbols such as light and darkness. Some are foreign to Biblical imagery, such as centering. A list of the symbols would be helpful at this point: light, darkness, centering, ascent, descent, fall, return, region of unlikeness, hierarchy. How these symbols fit together invites exploration of some platonic writers. Plato is the obvious starting point, but later Platonists such as Plotinus and Proclus were also influential on Christians. Plotinus in particular appears to have influenced Augustine, and Proclus appears to have been an inspiration to Dionysius the Areopagite.

Plato describes the philosophical quest of his teacher Socrates. When asked if he could teach virtue, Socrates answered that he would need to define virtues before being able to teach them (See *Meno* 71) He attempted to define such virtues as justice and piety. This quest for definitions of universal justice and equality appears to have contributed to the formulation of Plato's theory of ideas or forms.[6]

Socrates via Plato speculates that absolute standards including beauty, goodness, uprightness, and equality are beyond sense experience. From this he posits that these absolute standards predate birth. This absolute knowledge we lose at birth but recover it by recollection. Socrates sees that such objects of sense experience as two sticks are similar but not identical; this leads to a contrast between relative equality derived from senses to absolute equality, which derives from a realm of absolutes. (*Phaedo* 74-75) "So before we began to see and hear and use our other senses we must somewhere have acquired the knowledge that there is such a thing as absolute equality. Otherwise we could never have realized, by using it as a standard for comparison, that all equal objects of sense are desirous of being like it, but are only imperfect copies."(*Phaedo* 75b)

In the *Phaedo*, Socrates is presented by Plato as saying that we have a standard of absolute equality by which we judge all sense objects as imperfect. These forms or standards or ideals or ideas are not mere thoughts. These are "independent entities . . . always constant and invariable."(*Phaedo* 78d) Absolute beauty and goodness and the other forms exist, and a beautiful thing is beautiful because it "partakes" of absolute beauty. (*Phaedo* 100c)

This theory of forms helped to affirm a higher realm of existence and the interior human connection with that realm; Plotinus elaborates on this world view implied in this theory and provides Christian mysticism with a symbolic framework for spiritual experience.

Plotinus was born in Egypt around 204 c.e. and pursued philosophical study in Alexandria. He was inspired by a teacher there named Ammonius and stayed with him for eleven years. He journeyed to Rome and continued philosophical inquiry until his death in Sicily in 270.

There are three fundamental realities for Plotinus: the One, *Nous*, and *Psyche*. Everything emerges from the One; Plotinus uses the analogies of light and of water to conceive of the generation of others from the One. "The entire intellectual order may be figured as a kind of light with the One in repose at its summit as its King . . . we may think . . .of the One as a light before the light, and eternal irradiation resting upon the Intellectual Realm; this, not identical with its source, is yet not severed from it."(Plotinus. *Enneads* 5. 3. 12) " Imagine a spring that has not source outside itself; it gives itself to all the rivers, yet is never exhausted by what they take, but remains always integrally as it was [remains itself at rest]; the tides that proceed from it are at one within it before they run their several ways."(*Enneads* 3. 8. 10)

The One, sometimes called The Good, is beyond thinking as thought implies the duality of thinker and thought. The *Nous* or Intelligence emerges from the One by overflow. This emanation involves a looking back to its origin. The Nous or Intellective Principle has "traces of the Good" and is shaped into Goodness by the image of the Good upon it. (3. 8. 10) The Nous is the place of the Platonic forms. The Nous overflows to *Psyche* (Soul). A further overflow generates matter. These realities are a hierarchy of being in a stair step configuration. Plotinus also conceives of this hierarchy as a series of concentric circles with the One at the center and matter at the fringe. (6. 9. 8)

Emanation or procession emerges from the One, which he identifies as the Good. This emergence comes from the nature of the Good. "It is of the essence of things that each gives of its being to another: without this communication, The Good would not be Good, nor the Intellectual Principle and Intellective Principle, nor would Soul itself be what it is."(2. 9. 3)[7] This idea of the nature of the good to communicate itself carries into Christian understanding from Dionysius through to Bonaventure. This understanding of goodness in emanation brings ambiguity to Plotinus' understanding of emanation as it also involves a fall from unity. There is a degeneration in emanation as well as a communication from above. To speak of fallenness is best kept within the realm of the orientation of human consciousness.

Fallenness

Plotinus' dynamic point of view sees this emanation process involving a movement from unity to multiplicity. This effect of emanation or procession involves a lowering and a dwindling of intelligibility. "That Supreme pouring outwards comes at last to the extreme bourne of its light and dwindles to darkness."(4. 3. 9). Despite the language of "descent" Plotinus wants to maintain that emanation or creation does not mean failing:

> To those who assert that creation is the work of the Soul after the failing . . .of . . .its wings, we answer that no such disgrace could overtake the Soul of the All. If they tell us of its falling, they must tell us also what caused the fall.... We assert its creative act to be a proof

> not of decline but rather of its steadfast hold. Its decline could consist
> only in its forgetting the Divine. (2. 9. 4; see also 2. 9. 11)

Fallenness in the human being is a fall from center, a fall from likeness
to God, a fall into illusion from clarity. The fall leads to the region of
unlikeness, meaning unlikeness to God. "We are become dwellers in
the Region of Unlikeness, where, fallen from our resemblance to the
Divine, we lie in gloom and mud."(1. 8. 10)[8]

In Plotinus description of the cosmos is a setting for description of
the human psychological or spiritual situation. He writes about the
major principles of the world in order to contextualize the human
condition. Fallenness involves being lost in exteriority, that is to be
outside one's center looking for happiness.

> Let him who can, follow and come within, and leave outside the sight
> of his eyes and not turn back to the bodily splendours which he saw
> before. When he sees the beauty in bodies he must not run after them;
> we must know that they are images, traces, shadows, and hurry away to
> That which they image. (1. 6. 7)

Here Plotinus uses the Narcissus myth as metaphorical for this type of
alienation.

> For if a man runs to the image and wants to seize it as if it was the
> reality (like a beautiful reflection playing on the water, which some
> story somewhere, I think said riddlingly a man wanted to catch and
> sank down into the stream and disappeared) then let this man who
> clings to beautiful bodies and will not let them go, will, like the man in
> the story, but in soul, not in body, sink down into the dark depths where
> Nous has no delight, and stay blind in Hades consorting with shadows
> there and here.(1. 6. 7-8; English translation A.H. Armstrong. *Plotinus*
> (London: Allen and Unwin, 1953), pp. 136-137)

Return

The fall involves self-alienation through exteriority and through
forgetfulness of one's origin and true identity and self will. What can it
be that has brought the souls to forget the father, God, and though
members of the Divine and entirely of that world to ignore at once
themselves and It?

> The Evil that has overtaken them has it source in self-will. . .with the
> desire for self ownership. They conceived a pleasure in this freedom
> and largely indulged their own motion. . .they came to lose even the
> thought of their origin in the Divine.   . . .they misplace their respect,
> honoring everything more than themselves; all their awe and
> admiration is for the alien, and, clinging to this they have broken apart .
> . .Their regard for the mundane and their disregard of themselves bring
> about their utter ignoring of the divine.
>
> Admiring pursuit of the external is a confession of inferiority. (5. 1. 1)

Plotinus does not give the reader detailed methods of meditation but
rather symbols as pointers. The return to the One involves turning
within or centering. If one views the procession from unity through the
stair step (hierarchical) image, then returning means to go above which
is equivalent to going within in the concentric circle model. If the fall
involves self-alienating centrifugal force, then the return is centripetal
force in which one turns within to find peace and communion with the
Supreme. The erotic nature of the soul leads back to her origin through
longing and interiority.

> The soul in its nature loves God and longs to be at one with Him in
> the noble love of a daughter for a noble father; but coming to human
> birth and lured by the courtships of this sphere she takes up with
> another love, a mortal, leaves her father and falls.
> But one day coming to hate her shame, she puts away the evil of
> earth, once more seeks the father, and finds her peace. (6. 9 .9)

Fallenness involves a loss of clarity and a plunge into darkness; return
means to follow the beams of light above.

> Think of the traces of this light upon the soul, then say to yourself that
> such, and more beautiful and broader and more radiant, is the light
> itself; thus you will approach to the nature of the Intellectual-Principle
> and the Intellectual Realm, for it is this light, itself lit from above,
> which gives the soul its brighter life. (*Enneads* 5, 3. 8) [9]

The symbols of fall, return, region of unlikeness, centering, ascent,
descent, hierarchy, a God beyond the intellect, longing within the soul,
light and darkness all become the incorporated with biblical symbols in
later Christian writers. The language of such Platonists as Plotinus and
later Proclus become familiar in the spiritual writing of Augustine,

Gregory of Nyssa, Dionysius the Areopagite and many of those influenced in turn by them.

4. Gregory of Nyssa (ca. 335-395) Ongoing Growth, Divine Darkness; Dionysius: Hierarchy, Darkness, and Yearning.

In the name of acknowledging the encounter of Christianity and Hellenism I place together Dionysius the Areopagite and Gregory of Nyssa. They share numerous common symbols associated with hierarchy as well as a special reverence for darkness.

Gregory of Nyssa lived in the fourth century in southern Turkey, Cappadocia, a younger brother of Basil the Great. His spiritual writings show a love of solitude that led him to spend years in a monastery before becoming bishop. Whether or not he was married is uncertain. There is no reference to his supposed wife in any of his writings. The suggestion that he was married comes from chapter 3 of his treatise On *Virginity.* "Happy they who have still the power of choosing the better way and have not debarred themselves from it by engagements of the secular life, as we have, whom a gulf now divides from glorious virginity." If virginity here is understood literally, then Gregory may have been married. If it is taken as a technical term for virginity of the soul, then he may be lamenting his loss of purity by having become involved with secular life. [10]

Gregory's most important work is his *Life of Moses* in which he combines the biblical story of Moses with symbols of transformation adapted from Hellenistic culture to depict the spiritual journey. The method of distinguishing the historical (literal) meaning of the text from the spiritual meaning or allegorical meaning does not originate with Gregory. Both Philo and Origen before Gregory did their best to allow the symbolic meanings of the biblical text to carry them beyond the sometimes unacceptable obvious meaning to something more profitable for spiritual purposes. "If the events require dropping from the literal account anything written which is foreign to the sequence of elevated understanding, we pass over this on the grounds that it is useless and unprofitable to our purpose, so an not to interrupt the guidance to virtue at such points."(*Life of Moses* 2. 50; see the Introduction to *The Life of Moses.* Paulist Press, 1978, pp. 5-9.)

Whatever Gregory's marital state may have been, his love for the solitary life comes forth clearly enough in his treatment of Moses: "Separating himself from association with the people he thereafter lived alone. . .Moses lived alone in the mountains away from all the turmoil of the marketplace. (*Life of Moses* 1. 19)

From Virtue to Knowledge of God

Gregory identifies humans as self shaping. "We are in some manner our own parents giving birth to ourselves by our own free choice in accordance with whatever we wish to be"(2. 3) Those who live in peace and quiet will discover the rays of truth as sources of guidance. (2. 28) The combination of human discipline and "supernatural illumination" will lead the soul to great virtue. (2. 43) Virtue gives access to "the ineffable knowledge of God."(2. 152) The way to contemplation of God is purity (2. 154), and growth in virtue includes illumination from above. This developmental order corresponds to the classical language of purgation, illumination, and union. While Gregory does not use those exact words they are clearly part of *The Life of Moses.*[11]

He combines the Platonic and Biblical imagery of light and ascent. Where the Bible speaks of Moses physically going up a mountain and with literal light, the Platonized imagery speak of going to a higher state of consciousness by turning above or turning within ("deeper," 2. 163). The symbols seamlessly harmonize, and the biblical story becomes the story of the soul.

Darkness

The knowledge of God is ineffable because God dwells in darkness. Gregory speaks of darkness in two opposed meanings. The first darkness developmentally is ignorance from which religious knowledge gives escape: "the escape from darkness comes about when one participates in light." (2. 162) Here the receptivity to divine guidance and religious teaching gives a person who was agnostic an understanding of God's influence in life. This illumination gives way to a higher darkness, namely to a recognition and acceptance of God's incomprehensibility. "This is the seeing that consists in not seeing, because that which is sought transcends all knowledge, being separated on all sides by incomprehensibility as by a kind of darkness. (2. 163)

The movement from darkness to light to a higher darkness gives room for the positive contribution of religion as giving guidance and also of reverencing what is higher than itself.

Unending Progress

The divine darkness, which became such an important symbol for later centuries, suggests that as much understanding that Christianity has it nevertheless looks beyond itself to God as beyond the grasp of humans. This looking beyond has implications for Gregory's understanding of human spiritual progress. Since God is without limit so too is human progress.

> We hold the divine nature to be unlimited and infinite. Certainly whoever pursues true virtue participates in no other than God, because he is himself absolute virtue. Since then, those who know what is good by nature desire participation in it, and since this good has no limit, the participant's desire itself necessarily has no stopping place but stretches out with the limitless.
>
> It is therefore undoubtedly impossible to attain perfection, since . . .perfection is not marked off by limits: the one limit of virtue is the absence of a limit. How then would one arrive at the sought-for boundary when he can find no boundary?
>
> For the perfection of human nature consists perhaps in its very growth in goodness. (Prologue.7-10)

The person seeking God experiences the limitless of God through the unending desire to see God. (2. 239) Even the notion of contemplation has the dynamic understanding of pursuing the limitless: "the contemplation of his face is the unending journey accomplished by following directly behind the Word."(From his *Commentary on the Canticle of Canticles* quoted in the Introduction to *The Life of Moses* p.22).

Progress in virtue with its implied purification and guidance from divine light leads to a contemplative following, which means unending transformation.

Dionysius the Areopagite

The dates of Dionysius are unknown though twentieth century scholarship would like to associate his writings with the fifth century[12]; Gregory of Nyssa may be earlier than Dionysius as Gregory lived in the second half of the fourth century.

Dionysius is a pseudonym. In Acts of the Apostles (Acts 17:34) one named Dionysius who knew Paul appears, and this name was attached to a body of literature: *The Divine Names, The Mystical Theology, The Ecclesiastical Hierarchy, The Celestial Hierarchy*, plus ten letters. As a result of this pseudonym Christians invested this literature with enormous importance. The recognition of the false ascription to a contemporary of Paul came about in the late nineteenth century. Whether one calls the author Dionysius, Denis, Pseudo-Dionysius, or Pseudo-Denys, his writing is both influential and a good example of Platonized Christianity.

The mental framework of Dionysius includes the imagery of Platonism where the world emerges from the God who is beyond comprehension by the nature of the Good. Creation affirms that "the Good . . .extends Its goodness by the very fact of Its existence to all things."(*Divine Names* 4. 1) This world emerges by extension of Divine Goodness (which is synonymous with Divine Love) into hierarchies that are both spiritual and ecclesiastical. Many levels of angels emerge from God, and this procession continues into different levels of ministry within the church. The attractive power of the Good leads all people to return to God (*DN* 4.4.) This return to God aims at theosis.

> Theosis is assimilation to and union with God to the extent this is permitted. It is the common end of all hierarchy that a continual love of God and of divine things, carried out in a holy way in God and in unity, and previously, the total and irreversible flight from what opposes it, the gnosis of what is as being, the vision and the science of the holy truth, participation in God in uniform perfection and in the One Himself so far as this is permitted, the satisfying intuition that nourishes intellectually whomever tends towards it. (*Ecclesiastical Hierarchy* 1.4 quoted by Bouyer in *The Spirituality of the New Testament and The Fathers* (Desclee, 1960), p. 419)

What is clearer in Dionysius but contained in germ-like state in his Platonic predecessors is Divine Yearning. As we have seen above in

Plotinus, the soul is moved by eros and the world has emanated by the Good expressing its own nature. Dionysius gives center stage to this dynamic circulation by love in Chapter 4 of *On the Divine Names*.

> We must dare to affirm . . .that the Creator of the Universe Himself, in His beautiful and Good Yearning towards the Universe, is through the excessive yearning of His goodness, transported outside of Himself in His providential activities towards all things that have being, and is touched by the sweet spell of Goodness Love and Yearning, and so is drawn from His transcendent throne above all things, to dwell within the heart of all things, through a super-essential and ecstatic power whereby He yet stays within Himself.   Hence Doctors call him "jealous" because He is vehement in His Good Yearning towards the world, and because He stirs men up to a zealous search of yearning desire for Him, and thus shows Himself zealous inasmuch as zeal is always felt concerning things which are desired, and inasmuch as He has a zeal concerning the creatures for which he cares. In short, both the Yearning and its Object belong to the Beautiful and the Good, and have therein their pre-existent roots and because of it exist and come into being. (*DN* 4. 13)

Here we have a God who is not only Good and leaves traces of goodness in Nous (Plotinus), but this is Divine Eros who inspires eros within people. This is a God with a more than human heart despite all of the efforts of Hellenism to place God above emotion.   This is a world that is thoroughly graced where every movement to God comes from an inspiration from God's own Yearning.

Dionysius announces *The Divine Names* to be a theological work that deals with what people can know or say about God from Sacred Scripture. (*DN* 1. 1) The "hidden super-essential Godhead" is beyond all name and concept.   "It lovingly reveals Itself by illuminations corresponding to each separate creature's powers, and thus draws upwards holy minds into such contemplation (*theoria*), participation (*koinonia*) and resemblance (*homoiosis*) of Itself as they can attain."(1. 2) Since It is the cause, origin, and goal of all, the sacred writers celebrate It by every Name while they still call it "Nameless."(1. 5; 1. 7) The sacred writers draw their titles for the Nameless from "universal or from particular providences or providential activities" and from "heavenly visions."(1. 8) Dionysius' theological quest is inseparable from the mystical experience of Christians: "we press upwards to those beams which in the Holy Scripture shine upon us; wherefrom we gain the light which leads us unto the Divine praises"(1.3) While keeping in tact the Platonic imagery of radiating light and ascent to the One, Dionysius introduces reverence for Sacred Scripture and praise of God.

In contrast to the names of God derived from His manifestations through His activities, in *The Mystical Theology* Dionysius "Mounts upwards from below towards the category of transcendence, and in proportion to its ascent it contracts it terminology, and when the whole ascent is passed it will be totally dumb, being at last totally united with Him Whom words cannot describe. (*M.T.* 3) The contrast is not as obvious as one might assume as both works are filled with a sense of the unknowableness of God.   *The Mystical Theology* speaks of renunciation for the sake of ascent to the "divine Darkness: by the unceasing and absolute renunciation of yourself and all things, you shall in pureness cast all things aside, and be released from all, and so shall be led upwards to the Ray of that divine Darkness which exceeds all existence."(*M. T.* 1) The direction of the God beyond all concepts is to let go of all.   "The Darkness of Unknowing" is the height of experience for Dionysius (along the line of Gregory of Nyssa).   In that darkness the seeker

> renounces all the apprehensions of his understanding and is enwrapped in that which is wholly intangible and invisible, belonging wholly to Him that is beyond all things and to none else . . .. and being through the passive stillness of all his reasoning powers united by his highest faculty to Him that is wholly Unknowable, of whom thus by a rejection of all knowledge he possesses a knowledge that exceeds his understanding. (*Mystical Theology* 1)

Unknowing here becomes a way to God. Dionysius does not invent this negative path but gives expression to the type of awareness of the transcendence of God in which silence becomes a form of praise. Silence of mind and mouth witnesses to the limitations of a human in the presence of the unspeakable greatness of God.

5. Augustine (354-430): Autobiography

Augustine, though inspired by Platonism with such images as region of unlikeness, ascent, and illumination, is so much more than this inspiration that he deserves his own chapter. Augustine is probably the most influential Christian writer since New Testament authors. His best known work is the *Confessions*, which is not only a classic of Christian spirituality but also a classic of western literature. This was the first extensive spiritual autobiography and arguably superior to any of its type. While later autobiographies are as personally revealing, this first of its kind has never been surpassed in theological richness. Augustine manages to get beyond the usual self-effacing modesty of most Christian literature for a thousand years and bares his intellectual, moral, and spiritual struggles.

Confessions has two meanings in this book: (1) confession of sin and (2) praise or witnessing to God. To confess God is to profess belief in God, and much of the book is prayer directed to God.

Journey

Augustine does not idealize childhood; he finds sin operating throughout these years. He relates his greediness as an infant for milk and his mischievous stealing of pears from his pre-teen days. His adolescence and early adult years are given over to sensuality. "To Carthage I came, where there sang all around me in my ears a caldron of unholy loves. I loved not yet, yet I loved to love, and out of a deep seated want, I hated myself for wanting not. I sought what I might love, in love with loving and safety I hated, and a way without snares."(*Confessions* 3. 1)

His intellectual quest led him to Manichaenism, which he eventually discarded as inadequate to Platonism, which supported in him a non-material understanding of God. His sense of sinfulness fueled his search:

> You did turn me round toward myself, taking me from behind my back,
> where I had placed me, unwilling to observe myself; and setting me
> before my face, that I might see how foul I was, how crooked and
> defiled . . . I beheld and stood aghast and whither to flee from myself I
> found not. (*Confessions* 8.7)

Gradually, under the influence of the example of the hermit Antony of
Egypt and the preaching of Ambrose of Milan, Augustine found
himself responding to an inner voice, which asked him to take up the
New Testament and read.   In this simple act of faith, he found an
understanding of life and God that gave his restless heart some peace.
(See *Confessions* Books 6-8)

Augustine's famous lament is thoroughly Christian yet the language
resonates with Platonism:

> Too late have I loved You, Beauty so ancient and so new.   Too late
> have I loved You.   Behold You were within me and I was outside, and
> there I sought for you and in my ugliness I plunged into the beauties
> that you have made.   You were with me and I was not with you.   These
> outer beauties kept me far from you, yet if they had not been in you,
> they would not have existed at all.   You called, you cried out, you
> shattered my deafness; you flashed, you shone you scattered my
> blindness; you breathed perfume, and I drew in my breath and I pant
> for you.   I tasted, and I am hungry and thirst; you touched me, and I
> burned for your peace."(*Confessions* 10. 27)

The theme of exteriority versus interiority echoes perfectly the
Plotinian analysis of human alienation.   While Augustine uses Platonic
imagery, his journey is uniquely described not only by the detailed
personal information of the *Confessions* but also by the route his
journey takes.

The path of God for Augustine is by the exterior to the interior to the
superior.   These steps occur in the *Confessions* book 10.   Augustine
asks what is this God he loves.   He asks the earth, "and it answered, 'I
am not he.'"(10. 6) He turned within and explores his memory as a
"boundless chamber"(10. 15).   How much the memory contains, but
how did the memory come to contain the idea of God? "Where then did
I find You so that I could learn of you? For you were not in my
memory before I learned of you.   Where then did I find you, so that I
could learn of you?   I could only have found you in yourself above
me."(10. 26) Here Augustine uses the inward path as a way of pointing
to the need for grace.   He finds God in God.   God has come to him in

the simplicity of faith not as an object in the world or in his psyche. His life is altered by faith, and he places it above all intellectual activity. Augustine does not reject intellectual activity, but he subordinates it to faith. His often quoted statement "I believe in order that I may understand" (from *De Libero Arbitrio* 2. 2. 6) subordinates reason to faith and allows faith to enrich one's intellectual horizon. His intellectual journeys led him to look above.

Light and Illumination

Where Gregory of Nyssa and Dionysius are mystics of darkness, Augustine prefers to associate God with light. He uses light imagery in two different ways, one to describe mystical experience and the other to describe the knowing process.

The mystical element is a matter of a metaphor of vision:

> I entered into the innermost part of myself, and I was able to do this because you were my helper . . .and I saw with my soul's eye . . .an unchangeable light shining above this eye of my soul and above my mind. It was not the ordinary light which is visible to all flesh, nor something of the same sort . . . And you beat back the weakness of my sight, blazing upon me with your rays, and I trembled in love and in dread, and I found that I was far distant from you, in a region of total unlikeness. (*Confessions* 7. 10)

When Augustine speaks of seeing light he is in the realm of mystical experience. When he uses the language of seeing by illumination he is generally describing how God influences epistemology. Note how he uses the Platonic image of region of unlikeness here describing a metaphysical difference from God rather than the Plotinian moral difference. The other obvious difference from Plotinus is Augustine's acknowledgement of God as helper. Both the Christian transformations and the Platonic framework are evident.

Like Plotinus, Augustine uses light imagery for God and God's communication with humans. He transformed Plotinus' idea of reminiscence into illumination. The difference is where non-Christian Platonists accept a soul's pre-bodily communion with the eternal forms as a foundation for judgement. The remembering of knowledge from this prior existence is reminiscence. In Augustine God illuminates, that is, has a regulating influence on human knowing. "The judgement of truth from above is strong and clear and remains steadfast by the most incorruptible rules of its own right."(*On the Trinity* 9. 6. 10) Divine illumination tells a person what a thing "ought to be in the light of the eternal types."(*Trinity* 9. 6. 9)

Augustine locates the divine forms or ideas in the divine mind:

> For ideas are certain primary forms or patterns of things, abiding and unchangeable, not created, and therefore eternal and forever the same, contained in the divine mind; and whereas they themselves do not come into being nor perish, everything which can come into being perish, and everything which does not come into being and perish, is said to be formed according to them. (De *diversis quaetionibus* 83 section 46; this is quoted in Hans Mayerhoff's article "On the Platonism of St. Augustine's Quaestio de ideis" in *The New Scholasticism* 16: 1942, p.21)

For Augustine as for Plotinus to judge a thing beautiful requires the influenced of the form of beauty. For Augustine this comes into the soul from above by illumination in the present not a remembrance from a former existence.

Augustine writes about prayer in many of his works.[13] Generally he does not go beyond what the Bible says about prayer. In his *Letter 130* to a widow he repeatedly emphasizes that speaking in prayer is not so much to inform God as to rouse desire and motivation within oneself. In that latter he acknowledges the prayer of the monks of the Egyptian desert. This next chapter takes us into that world of desert spirituality.

6. John Cassian (ca. 360-432) and Benedict of Norcia (ca. 480-547): Desert Tradition

With an origin in the third century in the deserts of Egypt and Israel, the desert tradition began a long development of Christian monasticism. These men and women sought a religious intensity that an already conventional Christian culture apparently did not provide. Cassian relates early monastic life to the earliest church community in Alexandria.

> For in the early days of the faith few indeed . . .were regarded as monks . . .They not only retained then those magnificent qualities that we read in the acts of the Apostles (. . . one heart and one soul. . .all things were common to them. . .)but to these they even added things far more lofty. For they went off to quite secluded places on the outskirts of the city and led a strict life of such rigorous abstinence that even those who did not share their religion were astonished at the arduous profession of their way of life. For day and night they gave themselves over to the reading of Holy Scripture, to prayer, and to manual labor with such fervor that the very appetite for and memory of food only disturbed them every second of their day, when their bodies felt hunger, and they would take food and drink not so much out of desire as out of necessity . . .
>
> At that time . . . when the perfection of the primitive Church remained inviolate and was still fresh in the memory of succeeding generations, and when the faith of the few had not yet been spread among the multitude and grown lukewarm, the venerable fathers, . . . came together to discuss what form daily worship should take . . . (*Institutes* 2. 5. 1-3)

The sources do not offer a completely homogeneous desert life style, but most participants pursued union with God, combat with evil, prayer, manual labor (for survival and to keep the body healthy), reading of the Bible, compunction and purity of heart. The single best source for the early desert tradition is the work of John Cassian whose writing retains the color of the desert fathers, is practical and not overly philosophical and is not especially entangled in the miraculous. The monks he interviews exemplify withdrawal from ordinary society, solitude, silence, spiritual combat, transformation, and continual prayer.

John Cassian was born in Eastern Europe, perhaps modern day Romania; around 360 and traveled to a monastery in Bethlehem. He traveled to monasteries in Egypt and recorded the wisdom of the desert. He brought teachings of the Egyptian desert to Europe and established two monasteries in Marseilles. His influence is especially evident on the Rule of Benedict, which both recommends his writings and echoes his teaching.

The desert is a biblical symbol for an uninhabited place, and this symbol in the hands of the New Testament authors became a place for encountering God (John The Baptist calls people back to God in the desert.) and for combating temptation. The temptation accounts of Jesus in the desert in Matthew, Mark, and Luke show a parallel with the Israelite sojourn in the desert. The Israelites were in the desert for 40 years, hungered, and were tested (Dt. 8); the Israelites were collectively God's son (Ex. 4:22). In Exodus, the Israelites failed to remember God when tested and fell into complaining about God, putting God to the test by demanding water to come forth in the desert, and idolatry by worshipping the golden calf. Jesus as the new and improved son of God is 40 days in the desert but when tested, he remembers God and does not fall into those temptations associated with hunger, testing God and idolatry. Jesus' quasi historical experience ("quasi" because these events were taken as historical for the early Church though their historicity by contemporary standards is doubtful) becomes a source of inspiration for followers to put themselves in the lonely place of the desert and to combat evil in themselves and demonstrate their fidelity to God.

The writings of Cassian include *The Conferences* and *The Institutes*. *The Conferences* gives teachings on prayer, goals, evil spirits, discretion and the important inner realities of monastic life largely through interviews with desert dwellers. *The Institutes* give a long exposition on the recitation of psalms and on the eight principle vices.

Conference 1 sets out the goals of living in the desert, namely eternal life and the immediate goal of purity of heart, which gives access to the kingdom of heaven. Purity of heart which is synonymous with love of God (*Conferences* 1. 7. 1) implies effort to avoid any obstacles and to focus on God especially through solitude, readings, and fasting.

Solitude is an arena for combat with evil and with illusion. This struggle within oneself develops discretion or the ability to distinguish between right and wrong. (*Conference* 2) The discovery of evil or illusion in oneself leads to exposing the wrong thought or motivation to the light of day. "True discretion is not obtained except by true humility. The first proof of this humility will be if not only everything that is to be done but also everything that is thought of is offered to the inspection of the elders, so that, not trusting in one's own judgement one may submit in every respect to their understanding and may know how to judge what is good and bad according to what they have handed down."(*Conference* 2. 10. 1) This type of confession of one's thoughts implies obedience to a spiritual guide or at the very least to the wisdom of the Scriptures. Cassian (as later Benedict) also advocates obedience to all the members of the community even the young as the monk is "beginning afresh."(*Institutes* 2. 3. 2) Solitude with some association with others is a safer path than complete solitude. Cassian promotes the community (*cenobium*) for the sake of discretion.

Confession of one's thoughts is part of watchfulness of one's thoughts. (*Conference* 1. 17-20) Solitude gives the monk (Monks from *monos* applies to both hermits and those who live in community; all have a solitary orientation.) an environment where external distractions are minimized, and the inner gaze develops easily. Awareness of what the mind is doing and where it is leading give the attentive seeker some distance from acting on impulse, which is equivalent to an increase in personal freedom.

The awareness of sin or compunction (*Conference* 9. 26-31) which solitary pursuit of God discovers as a by product led the desert dwellers to discuss eight capital vices. These vices, which may borrow from Evagrius, nevertheless are not reducible to non-Christian sources. While the *Institutes* gives many pages to them, *Conference* 5 explores their relationship with one another. These are principal or capital vices because from them are born other vices. (*Conference* 5. 16. 1-5) The eight are gluttony, fornication, avarice, anger, sadness, acedia, vainglory, and pride.

> From gluttony are born overeating and drunkenness; from fornication—immodest speech, buffoonery, silliness, and foolish talk; from avarice—lying, fraud, robberies, perjuries, and desire for filthy lucre, false witness, violence, inhospitality, and greediness; from anger—murder, uproar, and indignation; from sadness—rancor, faintheartedness, bitterness, and despair; from acedia—laziness,

sleepiness, rudeness, restlessness, roving about, instability of mind and body, talkativeness, and curiosity, from vainglory—wranglings, heresies, bragging, and putting one's trust in novelties; from pride—contempt, envy, disobedience, blasphemy, murmuring, and slander."(*Conference* 5. 16. 5)

This daunting list comes along with a clear recognition that overcoming vices comes with the help of God. When the first six vices come under some control, the danger is that pride will become inflated as a result of some type of sense of achievement. The only hope is recognition of God in the process. (*Conferences* 5. 15.3-5)

Prayer

There are three basic types of prayer in Cassian: meditative reading of Scripture, psalmody, and repetitive prayer. Meditative reading of scripture is the same as "study" in the Benedictine tradition. This is reading that is spiritually transforming.

. . .you must strive in every respect to give yourself assiduously and even constantly to sacred reading. Do this until continual meditation fills your mind and as it were forms it in its likeness . . .containing in itself . . . constant steadfastness under the aspect of . . . a pure and sincere memory which preserve safely and lastingly . . . the enduring and heavenly sweetness of spiritual understandings . . .guarded by . . .the fullness of historical and spiritual knowledge . . .

Hence the successive books of Holy Scripture must be diligently committed to memory and ceaselessly reviewed. This continual meditation will bestow on us double fruit. First inasmuch as the mind's attention is occupied with reading and with preparing to read, it cannot be taken captive in the entrapments of harmful thoughts. Then, the things that we have not been able to understand because our mind was busy at the time, things that we have gone through repeatedly and are laboring to memorize, we shall see more clearly afterward when we are free from every seductive deed and sight, especially when we are silently meditating at night. Thus, while we are at rest and as it were immersed in the stupor of sleep, there will be revealed an understanding of hidden meanings that we did not grasp even slightly when we were awake.

But as our mind is increasingly renewed by this study, the face of Scripture will also begin to be renewed, and the beauty of a more sacred understanding will somehow grow with the person who is making progress."(*Conference* 14. 10-11. 1)

The reading of Scripture is the work of transformation not simply of collecting information. As such it is as much prayer as any activity.

The other forms of prayer are psalmody and repetitive prayer. Psalmody refers to singing or reciting psalms; in the cenobium this was performed communally seven times a day. This communal chanting of psalms comes from Jewish practice, the early Church and especially the monks gave themselves over to a practice that Jesus himself would have found in his own life. While some hermits may have gone through all 150 psalms in a day, the teaching of Cassian spells out seven times a day in such a way as to punctuate the entire day. (*Institutes* 3. 4. 3) The number of psalms at each time of prayer was in the vicinity of three.

The reading of psalms or singing of psalms involves listening to them, and there are two basic kinds of interpretations. The first type of reading allows the psalm to give expression to the monk's own experience (*Conference* 9. 29. 4); the second was a way of considering the experience of Jesus (*Conf*erence 9. 17. 1)

In conference 10 Cassian makes brief reference to imageless prayer and covers the topic of repetitive prayer. He notes the anthropomorphite heresy which ascribes a body to God as an obstacle to "that purest form of prayer which will not only mix no presentation of the Godhead or bodily contour into its supplication . . . but will indeed permit itself neither the memory of any word whatsoever nor the likeness of any deed nor a shape of any kind."(*Conference* 10. 5. 3) This type of prayer is cultivated by constant meditation on God. Ceaseless awareness of God is facilitated by repetition of a formula; the devotional formula he recommends is "O God, come to my assistance; O Lord make haste to help me."(Ps. 70:1; *Conference* 10. 10. 2) The repetition of this formula expresses desire for God and frees the practitioner from other thoughts. The formula is devotional in that it expresses longing for God; it is not simply a technique but presupposes as total gift of self to God as possible.

Progress: from Fear to Love

The journey to Egypt by Cassian and his companion Germanus was in pursuit of "a greater grace of perfection."(Conference 9.1) There Cassian interviewed an old monk named Chaeremon who spoke of fear: "There are three things that restrain people from vice—namely, the fear of Gehenna or of present laws; or hope and desire for the kingdom of heaven; or a disposition for the good itself and a love of virtue."(*Conference* 9. 6. 1) He then links these restraining forces with faith, hope and love. Faith gives access to dread of future judgement. Faith here is the opening to fear of "Gehenna". A pure materialist would not have to fear punishment; fear of this kind comes from faith. Hope for heaven moves the mind above vice. Love of Christ includes a love of virtue and is a way of imaging God. God loves as an expression of His own nature, and thus loves without thought of reward. The loving human has acquired a likeness to God by having a similar disposition toward goodness independent of fear and hope of reward; this disposition carries with it a pleasure in virtue. (*Conference* 11. 6. 1-2; 11. 7. 1)

Conference Eleven speaks of degrees of excellence or perfection meaning stages in spiritual development. The first degree is that of the slave who is motivated by fear; the second is that of the hireling who is moved by desire for reward. The third degree is that of the son who trusts in the generosity of his father. Fear is not something to be denied, but it is salutary. Fear helps to reorient a person, just as the hope of reward moves the person beyond earthly pleasure. The change of focus leads to a love whose only fear is that which belongs to a loving relationship, namely the fear of any offense against love. (*Conference* 11.13.1)[14]

Cassian is clearly a rich treasury of desert thought; when one turns to Benedict's Rule, it is difficult to find much in that Rule that is not contained in Cassian.

Benedict of Norcia

Benedict came from Norcia, a couple of hours northeast of Rome; he went to Subiaco, also near Rome, to become a hermit, but others flocked to him for wisdom. He created a Rule (*Rule of Benedict*, now commonly referred to as *RB*) that has been a foundation stone for m of subsequent monastic development in the west. After surveying Cassian and finding there the traditional Benedictine themes of psalmody, reading, manual labor, purification, obedience, and humility, the question arises as to what is the special contribution of *RB*? Surprisingly one of its greatest strengths is its brevity! In 73 short chapters *RB* is a guide to creating an environment for spiritual transformation. He says he is creating a rule for beginners and mentions the writings of Cassian and Basil as tools for virtue and sources of shame for those reading his rule. (*RB* 73) Benedict is not claiming to be an innovator; he is attempting to help people begin to live the monastic life.   The modesty of his language about writing a rule for beginners should not disguise the challenge of this lifestyle for a lifetime.

Fear and Obedience

The prolog sets the tone of urgency with the opening word: "Hearken, my son to your master's precepts and incline the ear of your heart. Receive willingly and carry out effectively your loving father's advice, that by the labor of obedience you may return to Him from whom you had departed by the sloth of disobedience." Listening is in service of obedience, which is the way of transformation.   The obedience mentioned in the prolog is the bedrock of the Rule and includes obedience to the Rule, to the Abbot (*RB* 7) and to the entire community. (*RB* 71) Obedience is also driven by "fear of hell" and hope of "life everlasting."(*RB* 5)

The prolog contains numerous references to fear as a motivator.

> . . . we must always so serve Him with the good things He has given us, that He will never as an angry Father disinherit His children, nor ever as a dread Lord, provoked by our evil actions, deliver us to everlasting punishment as wicked servants. . .

> Run while you have the light of life, lest the darkness of death overtake you.

> For if we wish to dwell in the tent of that kingdom, we must run to it by good deeds or we shall never reach it.

> . . . the Lord is waiting every day for us to respond by our deeds to His holy admonitions. And the days of this life are lengthened and a truce granted us for this very reason, that we may amend our evil ways.

> If we want to escape the pains of hell and attain life everlasting, then, while there is still time, while we are still in the body and are able to fulfil all these things by the light of this life, we must hasten to do now what will profit us for eternity.

> . . .if a certain strictness results from the dictates of equity for the amendment of vices or the preservation of charity, do not be at once dismayed and fly from the way of salvation, whose entrance cannot but be narrow. (*RB*, Prolog)

Benedict perhaps envisions a development from fear to love, but he does not spell this out very well. The prolog does speak of God as merciful and desiring to save sinners if they convert. Benedict's developmental hope in the prolog describes "our hearts expand and we run the way of God's commandments with unspeakable sweetness of love." Unfortunately, Benedict does not elaborate on the move from fear to love in the way that Cassian does.

Fear is actually a motivating factor behind forming community. Charity towards others Benedict ties to fear of hell.

> Just as there is an evil zeal of bitterness which separates from God and leads to hell, so there is a good zeal which separates from vices and leads to God and to life everlasting. This zeal, therefore, the monks should practice with the most fervent love. Thus they should anticipate one another in honor; most patiently endure one another's infirmities, whether of body or of character; vie in paying obedience one to another—no one following what he considers useful for himself, but rather what benefits another--; tender the charity of brotherhood chastely; fear God in love; love their Abbot with a sincere and humble charity; ...(*RB* 72)

However touching the descriptions of fraternal charity, *RB* links the impetus to such actions with choosing life with God versus life separate from God. Fear is an underlying motivation not only for ways of relating to the other members of the community; fear is also an underlying motivation for the conversion of life under the Rule.[15]

After the prolog the Rule describes the different kinds of monks, the abbot, instruments of good works, then a chapter on obedience, one on silence and a long exposition on humility. Silence for *RB* is a way to avoid sin. (*RB* 6)

Chapter 7 is a description of progress according to Benedict. He gives twelve degrees of humility beginning with keeping "the fear of God" before one's eyes. The second degree is that "a person love not his own will" while the third mentions obedience to the Superior. The fourth shows extraordinary progress in that the monk will "hold fast to patience with a silent mind when in this obedience he meets with difficulties and contradictions and even any kind of injustice, enduring

all without growing weary or running away." A silent mind is no easy
feat. Such deep acceptance even of injustice toward oneself is the mark
of one who has little ego left to protect. The fifth degree hearkens back
to Cassian in that the monk hid from the Abbot none of his evil
thoughts or sins committed. If one remembers the struggle with one's
Abbot may be a source for evil thoughts, to share these thoughts is a
deep path of reconciliation. There are other steps, which are
occasionally irritating to contemporary sensibilities, for example the
monk will "consider himself lower and of less account than anyone
else," and "he should always have his head bowed." One of the
dangers of such descriptions is to imitate outward behavior skipping the
implied interior change. A later follower of Benedict, Bernard of
Clairvaux in the 12th century, will give a more adequate context to
humility. The clearest theme of the chapter on humility is obedience.

RB gives a great deal of attention to psalmody. His treatment of
psalmody largely consists in designating what psalms are to be said at
what time; this shows the Rule to be a blueprint rather than a treatise.
The regimented way of life is in many respects monotonous. The monk
has little to think about concerning the arrangement of daily activities.
This monotony facilitates the inward turn that the *RB* seeks to create
through the monastic environment. Maria Montessori's notion of
prepared environments fits *RB* well. She noted that the entire life of the
honey bee is devoted to creating the best environment for the young
bees. *RB* is largely devoted to creating a context for transformation of
the monk's will.

The monk marks commitment to transformation in the monastic
community by taking vows. These are stability, reformation of life and
obedience. One finds reformation of life and obedience throughout the
rule. Stability deserves comment. Stability means local stability. The
monk commits himself to a particular place and particular community.
This community consists of people who will be sources of scandal and
annoyance, but learning to live in peace with this particular group of
imperfect people gives the Rule a rooting in concrete reality.

7. Bernard of Clairvaux (ca. 1090-1153): Love and Self-Knowledge

The Benedictine way of life flourished for centuries, and near the beginning of the twelfth century a small group of men wanted to reform that way of life. These Cistercians saw examples of Benedictine life where manual labor was absent from the monk's life, and monastic life had become softer than primitive desert monasticism of either Benedict or of Egypt. In 1098 in Burgundy, this group of men, (Robert of Molemnes, Stephen Harding, and Alberic) founded a School of Christ, later called the Cistercians. They attracted a talented and educated gentleman named Bernard who joined these early Cistercians with a group of his own friends and relatives. Bernard founded a monastery called Clairvaux and gave the monastic world some of its most developed thought on spiritual life. They did not have serfs as some of their Benedictine brothers; rather they insulated themselves from the local economic system by having laborers as part of the community.

Bernard's early works include *On the Steps of Humility* and *On Loving God.* Bernard of Clairvaux took the degrees of humility from the Rule of Benedict, gave the topic a definition of humility as truth, and proceeded to describe how to grow in humility. This growth involves an unavoidable confrontation with self and acquisition of compassion.

For Bernard of Clairvaux, humility is truth. The first degree of truth is the truth of oneself. Each person is an image of God, a creature, and a sinner. We either overvalue or undervalue ourselves by thinking we are center of universe or despicable. He would have people appreciate all of these dimensions. We are creatures; we have our feet in the humus. If the idea of humility is vague, consider the linguistic connection between humus, human, and humility. (Bernard does not relate humility to these three words.) We are made in the divine image; we are free, but we are not free from sin this side of the grave. To know that one is a sinner leads to efforts to reform. One can attempt to be severe with oneself, but still one will not reform that way. That kind of failure reemphasizes not only the sinfulness, but also one's need for God's mercy.

Thus truth of oneself leads to the second degree of truth, the truth of others. Truth of one's neighbors is that everybody else is in the same boat. Everybody is struggling with being faithful; everybody else is failing from time to time, and everybody depends on the mercy of God. Self-knowledge is the road to compassion. If one recognizes that other people are similarly struggling with same failures as oneself, then one will be able to commiserate with their misery and relate to their struggles. Unless one knows one's own sinfulness, one will look at others with disdain and will judge others. This freedom from contempt of others cannot easily be faked. Self-knowledge is the door to and foundation of compassion.

> The merciful quickly grasp truth in their neighbor, extending their own feelings to them and conforming themselves to them through love, so that they feel their joys or troubles as their own. They are weak with the weak; they burn with the offended. (*Steps of Humility* 3)

The third degree of truth is the truth of God. Compassion frees one from self-absorption and increases sensitivity to other people; these in turn help clear the way for increased awareness of God's love. Awareness of God's love is contemplation, which Bernard of Clairvaux describes as sweetness and resting in the presence of God. (*Humility* 7. 21)

This language of compassion gives richness to a purely instrumental view of community as support for solitude and even as sharing common activities and goals. Here the presence of the community gives a context for compassion. The community becomes a mirror for oneself and becomes an arena for going beyond oneself not so much by service of others as by compassion.

On Loving God

Another of Bernard's early works is *On Loving God*. This also charts spiritual development in terms of degrees. He begins by asking why and how God should be loved. He answers: "the reason for loving God is God Himself; the way is to love Him beyond measure."(*On Loving God* 1) To consider whom God is to recognize the truth in this statement.

Humans either have too low an opinion of themselves or too high an opinion. Humans are creatures (dependent), sinners (2. 4), and beloved images of God. (2. 6)

Bernard acknowledges that humans are governed by self-interest. A human being makes itself its own law, thus is slave to its own will, and the law of a slave is fear. (13. 36-14. 38) The true way of life is not lawless but is according to the law of God, which is charity in which self love becomes ordered. The right order is to love the body for the soul, the soul for God, and God for Himself. (14. 37-38). A human being begins with carnal or self-directed love; such is its likeness to the man of dust but develops into likeness to the heavenly man, Jesus Christ. (15. 39) The self-centered person is led to seek God by knowledge of oneself, which includes the insight that "one cannot subsist by oneself."(15. 39)

Bernard's answer to the bondage and fear of the slave is obedience to the common will, the eternal law. The common will is God's will accepted by the person willing to be a creature governed by the creator. (12. 36)

Bernard writes of liberation from self-centered living in terms of the development of four degrees of love. The slave fears for self and is motivated by fear in accomplishing apparently good deeds. (13. 34) This is the first degree of love: love of self for one's own sake. The person who is carnal may realize that it is right to share whatever goods one has with others. Bernard poses the question of what one would do "if while helping out your neighbor you find yourself lacking what is necessary for your life." In such a situation Bernard advises prayer to God who will provide (7. 24), thus in order to love another human being with perfect justice "one must have regard to God."(7. 25) The second degree of love is where someone loves God for one's own benefit as only God can keep one from sin and enable one to do good. (7. 25-9. 26) With frequent turning to God one develops an intimacy with God in which one tastes the sweetness of the Lord, and this sweetness entices one "more to pure love than the urgency of" one's needs. This is the third degree of love where one loves God for God's sake. (9. 26) The fourth degree of love is more elusive than the other three; I will use help from Bernard's *Sermons on the Song of Songs*.

Here one discovers oneself as "an altogether unworthy object even of your own love, except for the sake of Him without whom you are nothing." (*Song* 50. 6) One's miserable self, wandering in the land of unlikeness, a slave of self-will is not worthy of one's own love but for the fact of God's love. God's love which shines on the just and the unjust gives worth and reality to the sinner. After all without God's love, the sinner would not exist. Divine love is the basis for this enlightened self-love, but this basis contains a promise of transformation into likeness of God. Bernard counsels loving the sinner not for present nothingness but for what the sinner will become. (*Song* 50. 7) To love self for God's sake is the fourth degree of love. This love is in full recognition of one's inability to establish oneself in being (creatureliness) and of one's sinfulness, but also and more importantly such love for self includes awareness of God as source and end of self. This awareness can lead to fleeting moments where one may experience a loss of self-consciousness.

> To lose yourself, as if you no longer existed, to cease completely to experience yourself, to reduce yourself to nothing is not a human sentiment but a divine experience. (*Love* 10. 27)

To be so taken by God that one is taken out of self-consciousness—that is out of self-reflective awareness, out of watching oneself. To be so found by God that one is lost to oneself, is to reduce self to nothing, which means to diminish self-consciousness.

In his *Sermons on the Song of Songs*, Bernard affirms human freedom for the sake of loving intimacy with Christ the Bridegroom. Since Origen this Biblical love poetry has been a favorite with Christians, and Bernard writes 86 sermons on it.

I will highlight likeness to God rather than attempting to summarize all of the richness of these sermons. In Sermons 81 and 82, Bernard speaks of an indestructible and threefold likeness: "simplicity of essence," "perpetuity of life," "and "free choice."(81. 5-6) This threefold likeness is covered by the disguise of human deception, pretense, and hypocrisy. (82.2) Sin is stitched onto simplicity, death to immortality, and compulsion to freedom. The super-imposition of these evils upon the soul make it "unlike God and consequently unlike itself as well." He sees the likeness to God covered over as the soul subjects itself to slavery to sin. The unlikeness is voluntary while "the primal likeness remains."(82. 5) Unlikeness to God means unlikeness to one's truest self by becoming like a beast that is governed by its appetites.

In the state of sinfulness the soul sees that it "is not likely to imagine God to be like itself." Knowledge of sinfulness increases desire "to become its true self, simple and righteous, fearing God and turning from evil."(82. 6-7) Every person has the possibility of attaining to true likeness, which is charity, and to aspire to nuptial intimacy with the Word.

For Bernard, the true likeness to God is love, and love "absorbs and conquers all other affections." In loving embrace, identity of one's will with God's "makes of two one spirit."(83. 1. 3) Bernard sees the experience of awe and wonder as unimportant next to love; though one may honor and revere God, what he wants is love. (83. 4) Not only is the Divine Bridegroom Love, but also "love is the being and the hope of a bride."(83. 5)

For Bernard, loving union with God is the condition of the reformed likeness. "We are transformed when we are conformed."(62. 5)

Bernard also plays with the root "form" in his early treatise *On Grace and Free Choice*: Christ the image of the Father (Heb. 1: 3) is to reform the deformed likeness. He is the Form of the Father (Phil. 2: 6) that is the Wisdom of God who orders all things. Bernard draws the proportion: as all things are ordered by the Wisdom of God, so on the microcosmic level, free choice should govern the body according to righteousness. (*Grace and Free Choice* 10. 32-34)

In *On Grace and Free Choice* Bernard distinguishes between image and likeness. The image of God is indelible; it remains even after sin, as free will is intrinsic to human nature. Human freedom Bernard describes as freedom from necessity. What is lost is likeness to God, namely freedom from sin. . (7. 21) What humans have lost is the ability to "chose the licit as more suitable and reject the illicit as harmful."(4. 11) This free counsel or clarity of inner guidance is what humans have lost and what the gift of God will restore. (14. 49) What then of all of the monastic practices? The gift of God requires voluntary consent. Fasting, works of mercy and other practices are the path for reformation.

> Our intention, bent down under the weight of earthly cares, rises again slowly from depths to heights; the affection, languishing in fleshly desires, gradually gains strength for spiritual love; and our memory, sullied by the shame of former deeds, but now become clean once more with continual good works, reaches each day a new measure of joy. (14. 49)

For Bernard, spiritual reformation includes grace, effort, and loving intimacy with God. The transforming power of love under girds his lofty expectations.

8. Francis of Assisi (ca. 1182-1226) and Bonaventure (1217-1274)

The twelfth century saw the full flowering of western monasticism with Bernard of Clairvaux and his Cistercians. As Europe experienced population growth, the Church responded with attention to the pastoral needs of city dwellers. This began the period of the emergence of the mixed orders, that is orders devoted to both contemplation and pastoral action. Two of the more prominent religious orders of this type were the Franciscans and Dominicans. Along with urban growth came the development of universities, and theologians took up residence in the University of Paris to articulate their theological insights.

The most powerful spiritual person of this period is that of Francis of Assisi. Since he wrote very little, we are largely dependent on the writings of Bonaventure as his biographer and as third minister general of the Franciscan Order.

Francis of Assisi grew up as the son of a wealthy cloth merchant in Umbria. God called him away from the life of privilege to a life of service. His love of poverty, creation, and Christ crucified give his spirituality an unusual blend of Christ and nature centeredness. His Canticle of Brother Sun summarizes the family feeling he had for all of creation, and his reception of the stigmata show his devotion to Christ crucified.

Bonaventure, who was born just north of Rome in Bagnoregio, took the ideals of Francis and wedded these to academic study as a theologian at the University of Paris. He went on to lead the Franciscan Order and strove to be faithful to Francis' vision. He went so far as to return to the place where Francis received the stigmata before writing his spiritual masterpiece *The Soul's Journey into God.*

One of the few things written by Francis, Canticle of Brother Sun will lead to Bonaventure's interpretation.

Canticle of Brother Sun by Francis

Most high omnipotent good Lord,
Yours are the praises, the glory, the honor and all blessing.
To you alone, Most High, do they belong,
And no man is worthy to mention you.
Praised be you, my Lord, with all your creatures,
Especially Sir Brother Sun
Who makes the day and through whom you give us light.
And he is beautiful and radiant with great splendor,
And bears the signification of you, Most High One.
Praised be you, my Lord, for Sister Moon and the stars,
You have formed them in heaven clear and precious and beautiful.

Praised be you, my Lord, for Brother Wind,
And for the air—cloudy and serene—And every kind of weather,
By which you give sustenance to your creatures.
Praised be you, my Lord, for Sister Water,
Which is very useful and humble and precious and chaste.

Praised be you, my Lord, for Brother Fire,
By whom you light the night,
And he is beautiful and jocund and robust and strong.

Praised be you, my Lord, for our sister Mother Earth,
Who sustains and governs us,
And produces various fruits with colored flowers and herbs.

Praised be you, my Lord, for those who give pardon for your love
And bear infirmity and tribulation,
Blessed are those who endure in peace,
For by you, Most High, they will be crowned.

Praised be you, Lord, for our Sister Bodily Death,
From whom no living man can escape.
Woe to those who die in mortal sin.
Blessed are those whom death will find in your most holy will,
For the second death shall do them no harm.
Praise and bless my Lord and give him thanks
And serve him with great humility.

(translation by Ewert Cousins published in his *Bonaventure.* (N.Y.: Paulist
Press, 1978), pp. 27-28.

Francis addresses the ancient elements of air, fire, earth, and water; in psalm-like style he praises the Lord for the wonders of creation. The utterances of Francis show the antithesis of alienation, a man who even finds family feeling in death. Notice light "bears the signification of you, Most High One." This is at least a Biblical reference: "The sun of justice shall rise, with healing in its wings."(Malachi 4:2) Bonaventure takes this poetry and uses his Platonic framework to elaborate his notion of vestige, namely that God has left vestiges or imprints of Himself in creation.

From Bonaventure's *Life of Francis*

> Whenever he heard of the love of God, he was at once excited, moved and inflamed as if an inner chord of his heart had been plucked by the plectrum of the external voice. He used to say that to offer the love of God in exchange for an alms was a noble prodigality and that those who valued it less than money were most foolish, because the incalculable price of divine love alone was sufficient to purchase the kingdom of heaven. And he used to say that greatly should the love be loved of him who loved us so greatly. Aroused by all things to the love of God, he rejoiced in all the works of the Lord's hands and from these joy-producing manifestations he rose to their life-giving principle and cause. In beautiful things he saw Beauty itself and through his vestiges imprinted on creation he followed his Beloved everywhere, making from all things a ladder by which he could climb up and embrace him who is utterly desirable. With a feeling of unprecedented devotion he savored in each and every creature—as in so many rivulets—that Goodness which is their fountain-source. And he perceived a heavenly harmony in the consonance of powers and activities God has given them, and like the prophet David sweetly exhorted them to praise the Lord. (*Legenda Maior* 9. 1)

Here Platonism is married to the loving God who inspires spousal devotion. To see Beauty in Beauty Itself may come as easily from Augustine as Plotinus or Plato. The self-diffusiveness of the Good that we see in the fountain fullness of God echoes Dionysius. The spousal reference brings to mind Bernard of Clairvaux. What we see here is an interpretation of the experience of Francis in his joy in creation that joins this experience with the richest traditions of spirituality that preceded him. The genius of Bonaventure resides in his drawing together the threads of Christian spirituality into works that chart the paths to God. He does this most successfully in *The Soul's Journey into God.*

Francis' intense devotion to Christ crucified led to his reception of the marks (stigmata) of Christ in his own body. Bonaventure describes Francis' experience in his chapter 13 of the *Legenda Maior*:

> . . .while Francis was praying on the mountainside, he saw a Seraph with six fiery and shining wings descend from the height of heaven. And when in swift flight the Seraph had reached a spot in the air near the man of god, there appeared between the wings the figure of a man crucified, with his hands and feet extended in the form of a cross and fastened to a cross. Two of the wings were lifted above his head, two were extended for light and two covered his whole body

In the Prologue to *The Soul's Journey into God* Bonaventure returns to this same place, La Verna, where Francis received the stigmata and reflected upon the paths to God. He structures his work in terms of the three pairs of wings of the vision of the Seraph.

Each pair of wings represents one of three paths to God, namely the first pair refer to finding God through God's traces or vestiges in creation (chapters 1 and 2) Whether the magnitude of things or the multitude , the beauty, fullness, activity, or order that one sees in the world all lead to the same characteristics in God their source.

The second pair of wings (chapters 3 and 4) point to the image of God in the human soul. Here Bonaventure continues Augustine's alignment of powers of the soul such as memory, intellect, and will with the Father, Son, and Holy Spirit. Chapters five and six involve contemplation of God directly as being and as Trinity.

After these six chapters Bonaventure turns to a seventh way which he calls "mystical ecstasy" which expresses a turning "directly and intently toward the rays of light."(Prolog) In chapter 7 he quotes Dionysius in describing an experience of "superluminous darkness." In this single work Bonaventure draw together the Franciscan celebration of God through nature, the wisdom of Augustine on illumination and on the image of God in the soul, the spousal mysticism of Bernard(4) and the darkness of unknowing of Dionysius. All of these threads of tradition Bonaventure puts in the service of articulating paths to God. These are not merely speculative exercises but elements of itineraries in the soul's journey.

Bonaventure gives another way to God in his *Tree of Life.* Here the approach is the imagination. Bonaventure gives descriptions of scenes from the Gospels and invites the reader to enter the scenes.

> Embrace that divine manger; press your lips upon and kiss the boy's feet. Then in your mind keep the shepherds' watch, marvel at the assembling host of angels, join in the heavenly melody, singing with your voice and heart: Glory to God in the highest and on earth peace to men of good will.(*Tree of Life* 4)

The person meditating enters the scene of the birth of Jesus and evokes heart-felt devotion. Ignatius of Loyola in his *Spiritual Exercises* developed this method of relating to Christ in later centuries. (The approach of Bonaventure passed through Psuedo-Bonaventure and Ludolf of Saxony to Ignatius.) This imaginative approach demonstrates Bonaventure's devotion to the humanity of Christ in addition to his comprehensive synthesis of spirituality in *The Soul's Journey into God.*

The spiritually centered thought of Bonaventure had a parallel in more academic theology. In Bernard's time, Abelard had developed theology in a speculative manner by raising questions and giving the pros and cons of various answers. Thomas Aquinas, a contemporary of Bonaventure, followed that basic method, and his writing became the standard of theology for hundreds of years.

Thomas was daring in his embrace of the Aristotelian metaphysics, which he embraced as a young man in Naples. Aristotle provided Thomas with a new framework that, for example, grounded human knowing with no need for God. Bonaventure maintained divine illumination along the lines of Augustinian Platonism. While Bonaventure was cautiously open to Aristotle, he did not lose his mystical orientation.

During Bonaventure's academic career there were many debates about the place of Greek philosophy in Christian thought. He affirms the place of philosophy and all sciences in his *Retracing the Steps(De Reductione Artium ad Theologiam)* Even there he manages to refer to Christ as Spouse:

> The manifold wisdom of God which is luminously handed down in Sacred Scripture, is hidden in every act of knowledge and in every nature. It is also clear how all forms of knowledge are the servants of theology: wherefore this science assumes examples and makes use of expressions that belong to all kinds of knowledge. . . And such is the fruit of all science: in all, faith is built up, God is glorified, life organized, and consolations are provided, and all this is achieved through the union of the Spouse with the bride, accomplished by love: a love in which the whole of Sacred Scripture comes to rest, as also

therefore, every illumination from above without which all knowledge would be vain."(*Retracing* 26)

His unrelenting goal is to highlight the importance of Christian truth and of Christ as central or as pinnacle to all intellectual work and human action.

One may find some of Bonaventure's polemical writing against the dangers of Aristotle in his *Collationes in Hexameron.* Despite his openness to Plotinus and other "enlightened philosophers" he is critical of Aristotle's notions of eternity of the world and denial of Divine providence.(*Hexameron* 6. 2)   Even Bonaventure's favorite non-Christian philosophers "lived in darkness since they did not have the light of faith." Their vision and growth were less than adequate: "They had the wings of ostriches."(*Hexameron* 6. 24-7. 14) Without Christian faith philosophical knowledge will fail.

Though Bonaventure acknowledges philosophy's role as helping to build up the faith, he says the servant, philosophy, becomes a prostitute for those who choose her over Christ.(*Hexameron* 2. 7; 19. 18)

The highest manner of attending to God is by rapture and ecstasy, exemplified by Francis. Beneath this elevated state, Bonaventure places the Franciscans and the Dominicans, who with "clean minds" speculate upon Scripture. (*Hexameron* 22. 21) Rational theology as practiced by contemplatives he places on a high level, but it too is below the rapture of Francis. (*Hexameron* 19.3) Bonaventure as a professor was not against intellectual endeavor, but he remained above all a champion of the way to God beyond the sciences.

9. John Ruusbroec and Julian of Norwich: Fourteenth Century

In the fourteenth century numerous mystical writings appear. The devastation of the Black Death in Europe and Hundred Years War may have contributed to this inwardness. If the plague in Europe reduced the population by millions, surely people in a pre-scientific age would have intensified their religious fervor. Political instability generates discomfort and consequent religious interest. In addition scholasticism was taking religious thought into dry speculation that hardly nourished those longing for intimacy with God. Bishops were sometimes criticized for being overly concerned with wealth, and clergy were sometimes illiterate. Whatever the causes of this flourishing of mystical writings, the student has a rich menu from which to choose. In the Rhineland there are Meister Eckhart and John Tauler; two powerful voices of inward exploration. In Flanders John Ruusbroec can hardly be rivaled for beauty and clarity. In Italy the influential Catherine of Siena emerges. In England Walter Hilton, the author of the *Cloud of Unknowing*, and Julian of Norwich help to give the fourteenth century its reputation as a mystical era.

Two from this century that stand out are Ruusbroec for balance and Julian for charm.

John Ruusbroec (1293-1381)

Ruusbroec was ordained a priest in Brussels and served as a chaplain there for twenty six years. He left the city to live a more solitary life nearby in a greener setting at Groenendaal with two companions. Eventually they joined the Canons Regular of St. Augustine. He remained there for thirty two years until his death.

The two outstanding teachings from Ruusbroec's several works are the balance of activity and rest in God and the stages of spiritual life..

In his early and most important work *The Spiritual Espousals,* Ruusbroec describes activity and rest in God. These dynamics have obvious human implications. "The hidden divine nature is eternally active in contemplation and love as regards the Persons and is constantly in a state of blissful enjoyment insofar as the Persons are embraced in the Unity of the divine being."(*Spiritual Espousals* 3)

The activity of God is in part His creative activity: "This eternal going forth and this eternal life which we eternally have and are in God apart from ourselves is a cause of our created being in time."(*Espousals* 3. 3) The activity of God also occurs in God's expression of Himself in generation of divine Trinitarian Persons. God's nature involves an "eternal going forth" both in Himself and in creation. That going forth leads to an enjoyment as well as activity:

> In a way characterized by both activity and blissful enjoyment, the Spirit embraces and penetrates the Father and Son and all that lives in both of them with such great riches and joy that all creatures must remain silent before this, for the incomprehensible wonder which resides in this love eternally transcends the understanding of all creatures. . . .
> . . .here there is nothing other than an eternal state of rest in a blissful embrace of loving immersion.(*Espousals* 3. 4)

Creative and expressive activity in God lead to contemplative repose. As human persons bear the image of God, their experience contains the possibility of imaging these dynamics of God's life:

> It is to this eternal image and likeness that the Holy Trinity has created us. God therefore wills that we go out from ourselves into this divine light, supernaturally pursuing this image, which is our own life, and possessing it with him both actively and blissfully in a state of eternal blessedness.(3.3)

Ruusbroec thus finds inspiration for activity and rest in Christian inner experience in God's activity and rest.

Ruusbroec gives three stages of life in his *Spiritual* Espousals and adds a fourth in the *Sparkling Stone*. These stages are the Active Life, Interior life (or life of Yearning) and the Contemplative life. These first two are equivalent to stages used by Greek fathers and Desert Fathers, namely active life (*praxis*) and contemplative (*theoria*) life. There "active" refers to pursuit of virtue and self-purification; the contemplative life was a matter of *theoria*.

In Ruusbroec, the Active Life involves all that a person can do to purify self plus cooperation with God's grace. The virtues of obedience, renunciation of one's own will, patience, meekness, kindness, compassion, generosity, zeal, moderation and the like are the way of the active life. The cultivation of virtues is part of the life of faith in which the person has met Christ and is actively directing mind and will to Christ.(*Espousals* 1. 4)

The Interior Life implies that a person is free from inordinate attachments and is free of most images.(2. 1) The multiplicity of virtues now live in simplicity, meaning virtue does not end, but the grace of God makes virtue constant (2. 1. c) The purified person now may experience "the first coming of Christ" which "drives and urges on a person sensibly from within, drawing him with all his powers upward to heaven and pressing him to attain unity with God." Here a person feels the attraction of God. God's coming stirs yearning and interior restlessness and sometimes tears(2. 2/3. a) Interior consolations will be followed by a sense of abandonment as Christ withdraws his light and heat.(ibid.) The sense of abandonment by Christ gives the opportunity for the person to "place himself in the hands of God, rejoicing that he is able to suffer for God's sake."(ibid.) A second coming by Christ gives greater enlightenment to the person enabling the soul to see God's richness of God enabling the person to experience special joy and wonder.(2. 2/3. b).

A third coming of Christ generates an eternal hunger which can nevermore be satisfied." (ibid.) The soul continues to be blessed by gifts of understanding and love in the will.

The last stage in the *Espousals* is the "contemplative life." Ruusbroec here means a loss of self awareness as one is caught up in awareness of God. The person continues with virtue and but a new level of consciousness opens.

> Here there is a blissful crossing over and a self-transcending immersion into a state of essential bareness, where all the divine names and modes and all the living ideas which are reflected in the mirror of divine truth all pass away into simple ineffability, without mode and without reason. In this fathomless abyss of simplicity all things are encompassed in a state of blissful blessedness, while the ground itself remains completely uncomprehended . . .here there is nothing other than an eternal state of rest in a blissful embrace of loving immersion.(3. 4)

From active pursuit of God through virtue opens a sense of loving God and being loved by Him to a blissful state of rest. To this development

Ruusbroec adds another in *The Sparkling Stone* also written prior to his move to Groenendaal.

The person who undergoes transformation via faith and virtue and loving intimacy and ecstatic union with God is returned to the community. This person is available to the needs of others, and this person has an inexhaustible source of energy that will never be drained.(*Sparkling Stone*, conclusion) Ruusbroec's rhythm of action and contemplation here situates the transformed person at the service of the needs of others.

Julian of Norwich (ca. 1342--1416): Divine Motherhood

Julian is perhaps the most unique voice of the 14th century Christian tradition. Julian was a hermit who lived in a cell attached to a church in Norwich. Her writings though not particularly popular in her day have come to be a must read for contemporary students particularly as a result of the development of feminism in Christian circles.

What one finds in Julian's *Revelations* are descriptions of visions and theological and spiritual reflections that stem from these visionary experiences.

Julian, born in 1342, most likely received revelations in 1373 in which she wrote the short version of her *Revelations*. The Long text came twenty years later and contain more extended theological reflections.[16]

The visions themselves are problematic for readers inasmuch as most people do not have visions upon which to base their spiritual life. The second problem is these visions can be bloody. "I saw blood running down from under the crown, hot and flowing freely and copiously, a living stream, just as it was at the time when the crown of thorns was pressed on his blessed head."(*Revelations*, Long Text ch. 4). The genius of Julian is to find in the bloody depictions God's comfort and ultimately joy.

Joy

Julian does not shrink from the suffering of Christ, but she manages to discover there love and tenderness and joy in God's love. This may be her real appeal. Julian is charming with her joyfulness and her window on the tender mercies of God. If one is touched by the parental love of the Sermon on the Mount where God will clothe and feed his children, Julian gives page after page of discovery and rediscovery of the courtesy of God who shares His joy. Immediately after the bloody scene Julian proclaims the joy filling her heart comes from the Trinity who is "protector. . .everlasting lover. . . and endless joy and our bliss"(ibid.)

> At the same time as I saw this sight of the head bleeding, our good Lord showed a spiritual sight of his familiar love. I saw that he is to us everything which is good and comforting for your help. He is our clothing, who wraps and enfolds us for love, embraces us and shelters us, surrounds us for his love, which is so tender that he may never desert us.
> God wishes to be known, and it pleases him that we should rest in him.(*Revelations*, Long text ch. 5).

The joy of God and the joy in God are never far from any page of her writing. This is an extended source of consolation for the faithful.

Motherhood of God

Her depiction of God and Christ as motherly fit overall focus on care and joy. This emphasis is not her creation; in the New Testament Jesus is depicted as using motherly imagery of his care and concern for people. "How often would I have gathered your children together as a hen gathers her brood under her wings."(Luke 13: 39) This motherly utterance of Jesus is accompanied by expression of his prophetic condemnation of the people who would not accept the prophets. Julian takes motherly expressions and applies them to the Trinity, namely Christ as Second Person of the Trinity who takes on human nature out of maternal care.

> I saw that the second person, who is our Mother, substantially the same beloved person, has now become our mother sensually, because we are double by God's creating, that is to say substantial and sensual. Our substance is the higher part, which we have in our Father, God almighty; and the second person of the Trinity is our mother in nature in our substantial creation, in whom we are founded and rooted, and he is our Mother of mercy in taking our sensuality. And so our Mother is working in us in various ways, in him our parts are kept undivided; for in our Mother Christ we profit and increase, and in mercy he reforms and restores us, and by the power of his Passion, his death and his Resurrection he unites us to our substance. So our mother works in

mercy on all his beloved children who are docile and obedient to him.
(*Revelations*, Long text 58)

If this distinction of creation by the Father and the Mother is nebulous,
Julian goes on to clarify: "thus in our Father, God almighty, we have
our being, and in our mother of mercy we have our reforming and our
restoring."(ibid.)

All of the ready care and willingness to sacrifice of motherhood here
find expression in Jesus. The sharp edge of the prophet from Nazareth
is here made less stinging by motherly imagery. Julian does not deny
sinfulness, but she consistently finds joy in seeing the lengths to which
God has gone in order to embrace sinners: Whatever the pain caused
by sin, she is unfaltering in affirming that "all will be well, and every
kind of thing will be well."(ch. 27)

Julian's influence has been less than the greatest of Christian writers,
but her joyful voice is worth hearing especially her celebration of joy in
the hearts of God and His children.

Spirituality Anthology

10. Bible Selections

1: "All the commandment which I command you this day you shall be careful to do, that you may live and multiply, and go in and possess the land which the LORD swore to give to your fathers.

2: And you shall remember all the way which the LORD your God has led you these forty years in the wilderness, that he might humble you, testing you to know what was in your heart, whether you would keep his commandments, or not.

3: And he humbled you and let you hunger and fed you with manna, which you did not know, nor did your fathers know; that he might make you know that man does not live by bread alone, but that man lives by everything that proceeds out of the mouth of the LORD.

4: Your clothing did not wear out upon you, and your foot did not swell, these forty years.

5: Know then in your heart that, as a man disciplines his son, the LORD your God disciplines you.

6: So you shall keep the commandments of the LORD your God, by walking in his ways and by fearing him.

7: For the LORD your God is bringing you into a good land, a land of brooks of water, of fountains and springs, flowing forth in valleys and hills,

8: a land of wheat and barley, of vines and fig trees and pomegranates, a land of olive trees and honey,

9: a land in which you will eat bread without scarcity, in which you will lack nothing, a land whose stones are iron, and out of whose hills you can dig copper.

10: And you shall eat and be full, and you shall bless the LORD your God for the good land he has given you.

11: "Take heed lest you forget the LORD your God, by not keeping his commandments and his ordinances and his statutes, which I command you this day:

12: lest, when you have eaten and are full, and have built goodly houses and live in them,

13: and when your herds and flocks multiply, and your silver and gold is multiplied, and all that you have is multiplied,

14: then your heart be lifted up, and you forget the LORD your God, who brought you out of the land of Egypt, out of the house of bondage,

15: who led you through the great and terrible wilderness, with its fiery serpents and scorpions and thirsty ground where there was no water, who brought you water out of the flinty rock,

16: who fed you in the wilderness with manna which your fathers did not know, that he might humble you and test you, to do you good in the end

17: Beware lest you say in your heart, `My power and the might of my hand have gotten me this wealth.'

18: You shall remember the LORD your God, for it is he who gives you power to get wealth; that he may confirm his covenant which he swore to your fathers, as at this day.

19: And if you forget the LORD your God and go after other gods and serve them and worship them, I solemnly warn you this day that you shall surely perish.

20: Like the nations that the LORD makes to perish before you, so shall you perish, because you would not obey the voice of the LORD your God.

Deuteronomy, Chapter 8, RSV

8: The voice of my beloved! Behold, he comes, leaping upon the mountains, bounding over the hills.

9: My beloved is like a gazelle, or a young stag. Behold, there he stands behind our wall, gazing in at the windows, looking through the lattice.

10: My beloved speaks and says to me: "Arise, my love, my fair one, and come away;

11: for lo, the winter is past, the rain is over and gone.

12: The flowers appear on the earth, the time of singing has come, and the voice of the turtledove is heard in our land.

13: The fig tree puts forth its figs, and the vines are in blossom; they give forth fragrance. Arise, my love, my fair one, and come away.

14: O my dove, in the clefts of the rock, in the covert of the cliff, let me see your face, let me hear your voice, for your voice is sweet, and your face is comely.

From Song of Songs Chapter 2

1: Upon my bed by night I sought him whom my soul loves; I sought him, but found him not; I called him, but he gave no answer.
2: "I will rise now and go about the city, in the streets and in the squares; I will seek him whom my soul loves." I sought him, but found him not.
3: The watchmen found me, as they went about in the city. "Have you seen him whom my soul loves?"
4: Scarcely had I passed them, when I found him whom my soul loves. I held him, and would not let him go until I had brought him into my mother's house, and into the chamber of her that conceived me.

From Song of Songs Chapter 3

9: You have ravished my heart, my sister, my bride, you have ravished my heart with a glance of your eyes, with one jewel of your necklace.
10: How sweet is your love, my sister, my bride! how much better is your love than wine, and the fragrance of your oils than any spice!

From Song of Songs Chapter 4

1: In those days, when again a great crowd had gathered, and they had nothing to eat, he called his disciples to him, and said to them,
2: "I have compassion on the crowd, because they have been with me now three days, and have nothing to eat;
3: and if I send them away hungry to their homes, they will faint on the way; and some of them have come a long way."
4: And his disciples answered him, "How can one feed these men with bread here in the desert?"
5: And he asked them, "How many loaves have you?" They said, "Seven."
6: And he commanded the crowd to sit down on the ground; and he took the seven loaves, and having given thanks he broke them and gave them to his disciples to set before the people; and they set them before the crowd.

7: And they had a few small fish; and having blessed them, he commanded that these also should be set before them.

8: And they ate, and were satisfied; and they took up the broken pieces left over, seven baskets full.

9: And there were about four thousand people.

10: And he sent them away; and immediately he got into the boat with his disciples, and went to the district of Dalmanu'tha.

11: The Pharisees came and began to argue with him, seeking from him a sign from heaven, to test him.

12: And he sighed deeply in his spirit, and said, "Why does this generation seek a sign? Truly, I say to you, no sign shall be given to this generation."

13: And he left them, and getting into the boat again he departed to the other side.

14: Now they had forgotten to bring bread; and they had only one loaf with them in the boat.

15: And he cautioned them, saying, "Take heed, beware of the leaven of the Pharisees and the leaven of Herod."

16: And they discussed it with one another, saying, "We have no bread."

17: And being aware of it, Jesus said to them, "Why do you discuss the fact that you have no bread? Do you not yet perceive or understand? Are your hearts hardened?

18: Having eyes do you not see, and having ears do you not hear? And do you not remember?

19: When I broke the five loaves for the five thousand, how many baskets full of broken pieces did you take up?" They said to him, "Twelve."

20: "And the seven for the four thousand, how many baskets full of broken pieces did you take up?" And they said to him, "Seven."

21: And he said to them, "Do you not yet understand?"

22: And they came to Beth-sa'ida. And some people brought to him a blind man, and begged him to touch him.

23: And he took the blind man by the hand, and led him out of the village; and when he had spit on his eyes and laid his hands upon him, he asked him, "Do you see anything?"

24: And he looked up and said, "I see men; but they look like trees, walking."

25: Then again he laid his hands upon his eyes; and he looked intently and was restored, and saw everything clearly.

26: And he sent him away to his home, saying, "Do not even enter the village."

27: And Jesus went on with his disciples, to the villages of Caesare'a Philip'pi; and on the way he asked his disciples, "Who do men say that I am?"

28: And they told him, "John the Baptist; and others say, Eli'jah; and others one of the prophets."

29: And he asked them, "But who do you say that I am?" Peter answered him, "You are the Christ."

30: And he charged them to tell no one about him.

31: And he began to teach them that the Son of man must suffer many things, and be rejected by the elders and the chief priests and the scribes, and be killed, and after three days rise again.

32: And he said this plainly. And Peter took him, and began to rebuke him.

33: But turning and seeing his disciples, he rebuked Peter, and said, "Get behind me, Satan! For you are not on the side of God, but of men."

34: And he called to him the multitude with his disciples, and said to them, "If any man would come after me, let him deny himself and take up his cross and follow me.

35: For whoever would save his life will lose it; and whoever loses his life for my sake and the gospel's will save it.

36: For what does it profit a man, to gain the whole world and forfeit his life?

37: For what can a man give in return for his life?

38: For whoever is ashamed of me and of my words in this adulterous and sinful generation, of him will the Son of man also be ashamed, when he comes in the glory of his Father with the holy angels."

Gospel According to Mark Chapter 8

1: When Jesus had spoken these words, he lifted up his eyes to heaven and said, "Father, the hour has come; glorify thy Son that the Son may glorify thee,

2: since thou hast given him power over all flesh, to give eternal life to all whom thou hast given him.

3: And this is eternal life, that they know thee the only true God, and Jesus Christ whom thou hast sent.

4: I glorified thee on earth, having accomplished the work which thou gavest me to do;

5: and now, Father, glorify thou me in thy own presence with the glory which I had with thee before the world was made.

6: "I have manifested thy name to the men whom thou gavest me out of the world; thine they were, and thou gavest them to me, and they have kept thy word.

7: Now they know that everything that thou hast given me is from thee;

8: for I have given them the words which thou gavest me, and they have received them and know in truth that I came from thee; and they have believed that thou didst send me.

9: I am praying for them; I am not praying for the world but for those whom thou hast given me, for they are thine;

10: all mine are thine, and thine are mine, and I am glorified in them.

11: And now I am no more in the world, but they are in the world, and I am coming to thee. Holy Father, keep them in thy name, which thou hast given me, that they may be one, even as we are one.

12: While I was with them, I kept them in thy name, which thou hast given me; I have guarded them, and none of them is lost but the son of perdition, that the scripture might be fulfilled.

13: But now I am coming to thee; and these things I speak in the world, that they may have my joy fulfilled in themselves.

14: I have given them thy word; and the world has hated them because they are not of the world, even as I am not of the world.

15: I do not pray that thou shouldst take them out of the world, but that thou shouldst keep them from the evil one.

16: They are not of the world, even as I am not of the world.

17: Sanctify them in the truth; thy word is truth.

18: As thou didst send me into the world, so I have sent them into the world.

19: And for their sake I consecrate myself, that they also may be consecrated in truth.

20: "I do not pray for these only, but also for those who believe in me through their word,

21: that they may all be one; even as thou, Father, art in me, and I in thee, that they also may be in us, so that the world may believe that thou hast sent me.

22: The glory which thou hast given me I have given to them, that they may be one even as we are one,

23: I in them and thou in me, that they may become perfectly one, so that the world may know that thou hast sent me and hast loved them even as thou hast loved me.

24: Father, I desire that they also, whom thou hast given me, may be with me where I am, to behold my glory which thou hast given me in thy love for me before the foundation of the world.

25: O righteous Father, the world has not known thee, but I have known thee; and these know that thou hast sent me.

26: I made known to them thy name, and I will make it known, that the love with which thou hast loved me may be in them, and I in them."

The Gospel according to John Chapter 17

1: Therefore, having this ministry by the mercy of God, we do not lose heart.

2: We have renounced disgraceful, underhanded ways; we refuse to practice cunning or to tamper with God's word, but by the open statement of the truth we would commend ourselves to every man's conscience in the sight of God.

3: And even if our gospel is veiled, it is veiled only to those who are perishing.

4: In their case the god of this world has blinded the minds of the unbelievers, to keep them from seeing the light of the gospel of the glory of Christ, who is the likeness of God.

5: For what we preach is not ourselves, but Jesus Christ as Lord, with ourselves as your servants for Jesus' sake.

6: For it is the God who said, "Let light shine out of darkness," who has shone in our hearts to give the light of the knowledge of the glory of God in the face of Christ.

7: But we have this treasure in earthen vessels, to show that the transcendent power belongs to God and not to us.

8: We are afflicted in every way, but not crushed; perplexed, but not driven to despair;

9: persecuted, but not forsaken; struck down, but not destroyed;

10: always carrying in the body the death of Jesus, so that the life of Jesus may also be manifested in our bodies.

11: For while we live we are always being given up to death for Jesus' sake, so that the life of Jesus may be manifested in our mortal flesh.

12: So death is at work in us, but life in you.

13: Since we have the same spirit of faith as he had who wrote, "I believed, and so I spoke," we too believe, and so we speak,

14: knowing that he who raised the Lord Jesus will raise us also with Jesus and bring us with you into his presence.

15: For it is all for your sake, so that as grace extends to more and more people it may increase thanksgiving, to the glory of God.

16: So we do not lose heart. Though our outer nature is wasting away, our inner nature is being renewed every day.

17: For this slight momentary affliction is preparing for us an eternal weight of glory beyond all comparison,

18: because we look not to the things that are seen but to the things that are unseen; for the things that are seen are transient, but the things that are unseen are eternal.

Paul's Second Letter to the Corinthians Chapter 4

11. Clement of Alexandria Selections

On Prayer

Having got to this point, I recollect the doctrines about there being no necessity to pray, introduced by certain of the heterodox, that is, the followers of the heresy of Prodicus. That they may not then be inflated with conceit about this godless wisdom of theirs, as if it were strange, let them learn that it was embraced before by the philosophers called Cyrenaics. Nevertheless, the unholy knowledge (*gnosis*) of those falsely called [Gnostics] shall meet with confutation at a fitting time; so that the assault on them, by no means brief, may not, by being introduced into the commentary, break the discourse in hand, in which we are showing that the only really holy and pious man is he who is truly a Gnostic according to the rule of the Church, to whom alone the petition made in accordance with the will of God is granted, on asking and on thinking. For as God can do all that He wishes, so the Gnostic receives all that he asks. For, universally, God knows those who are and those who are not worthy of good things; whence He gives to each what is suitable. Wherefore to those that are unworthy, though they ask often, He will not give; but He will give to those who are worthy.

Nor is petition superfluous, though good things are given without claim.

Now thanksgiving and request for the conversion of our neighbours is the function of the Gnostic; as also the Lord prayed, giving thanks for the accomplishment of His ministry, praying that as many as possible might attain to knowledge; that in the saved, by salvation, through knowledge, God might be glorified, and He who is alone good and alone Saviour might be acknowledged through the Son from age to age. But also faith, that one will receive, is a species of prayer gnostically laid up in store.

But if any occasion of converse with God becomes prayer, no opportunity of access to God ought to be omitted. Without doubt, the holiness of the Gnostic, in union with [God's] blessed Providence, exhibits in voluntary confession the perfect beneficence of God. For the holiness of the Gnostic, and the reciprocal benevolence of the friend of God, are a kind of corresponding movement of providence. For neither is God involuntarily good, as the fire is warming; but in Him the imparting of good things is voluntary, even if He receive the request previously.

From Book 7, *Stromata*

For knowledge (*gnosis*), to speak generally, a perfecting of man as man, is consummated by acquaintance with divine things, in character, life, and word, accordant and conformable to itself and to the divine Word. For by it faith is perfected, inasmuch as it is solely by it that the believer becomes perfect. Faith is an internal good, and without searching for God, confesses His existence, and glorifies Him as existent. Whence by starting from this faith, and being developed by it, through the grace of God, the knowledge respecting Him is to be acquired as far as possible.

Now we assert that knowledge (*gnosis*) differs from the wisdom (σοφια), which is the result of teaching. For as far as anything is knowledge, so far is it certainly wisdom; but in as far as aught is wisdom, it is not certainly knowledge. For the term wisdom appears only in the knowledge of the uttered word.

But it is not doubting in reference to God, but believing, that is the foundation of knowledge. But Christ is both the foundation and the superstructure, by whom are both the beginning and the ends. And the extreme points, the beginning and the end -- I mean faith and love -- are not taught. But knowledge, conveyed from communication through the grace of God as a deposit, is entrusted to those who show themselves worthy of it; and from it the worth of love beams forth from light to light. For it is said, "To him that hath shall be given:" to faith, knowledge; and to knowledge, love; and to love, the inheritance.

And this takes place, whenever one hangs on the Lord by faith, by knowledge, by love, and ascends along with Him to where the God and guard of our faith and love is. Whence at last (on account of the necessity for very great preparation and previous training in order both to hear what is said, and for the composure of life, and for advancing intelligently to a point beyond the righteousness of the law) it is that knowledge is committed to those fit and selected for it. It leads us to the endless and perfect end, teaching us beforehand the future life that we shall lead, according to God, and with gods; after we are freed from all punishment and penalty which we undergo, in consequence of our sins, for salutary discipline. After which redemption the reward and the honours are assigned to those who have become perfect; when they have got done with purification, and ceased from all service, though it be holy service, and among saints. Then become pure in heart, and near to the Lord, there awaits them restoration to everlasting contemplation; and they are called by the appellation of gods, being destined to sit on thrones with the other gods that have been first put in their places by the Saviour.

Knowledge is therefore quick in purifying, and fit for that acceptable transformation to the better. Whence also with ease it removes [the soul] to what is akin to the soul, divine and holy, and by its own light conveys man through the mystic stages of advancement; till it restores the pure in heart to the crowning place of rest; teaching to gaze on God, face to face, with knowledge and comprehension. For in this consists the perfection of the gnostic soul, in its being with the Lord, where it is in immediate subjection to Him, after rising above all purification and service.

Faith is then, so to speak, a comprehensive knowledge of the essentials; and knowledge is the strong and sure demonstration of what is received by faith, built upon faith by the Lord's teaching, conveying [the soul] on to infallibility, science, and comprehension. And, in my view, the first saving change is that from heathenism to faith, as I said before; and the second, that from faith to knowledge. And the latter terminating in love, thereafter gives the loving to the loved, that which knows to that which is known. And, perchance, such an one has already attained the condition of "being equal to the angels." Accordingly, after the highest excellence in the flesh, changing always duly to the better, he urges his flight to the ancestral hall, through the holy septenniad [of heavenly abodes] to the Lord's own mansion; to be a light, steady, and continuing eternally, entirely and in every part immutable.

From Book 7, Chapter 10. William Wilson, Translator *The Writings of Clement of Alexandria: The Miscellanies,* Vol. 12 of The Ante-Nicene Christian Library copyright © 1872 by T. &T. Clark 1872, 446-448.

12. Platonism Selections

Plotinus

8. But what must we do? How lies the path? How come to vision of the inaccessible Beauty, dwelling as if in consecrated precincts, apart from the common ways where all may see, even the profane? He that has the strength, let him arise and withdraw into himself, foregoing all that is known by the eyes, turning away for ever from the material beauty that once made his joy. When he perceives those shapes of grace that show in body, let him not pursue: he must know them for copies, vestiges, shadows, and hasten away towards That they tell of. For if anyone follow what is like a beautiful shape playing over water- is there not a myth telling in symbol of such a dupe, how he sank into the depths of the current and was swept away to nothingness? So too, one that is held by material beauty and will not break free shall be precipitated, not in body but in Soul, down to the dark depths loathed of the Intellective-Being, where, blind even in the Lower-World, he shall have commerce only with shadows, there as here.

"Let us flee then to the beloved Fatherland": this is the soundest counsel. But what is this flight? How are we to gain the open sea? For Odysseus is surely a parable to us when he commands the flight from the sorceries of Circe or Calypso- not content to linger for all the pleasure offered to his eyes and all the delight of sense filling his days.

The Fatherland to us is There whence we have come, and There is The Father.

What then is our course, what the manner of our flight? This is not of a journey for the feet; the feet bring us only from land to land; nor need you think of coach or ship to carry you away; all this order of things you must set aside and refuse to see: you must close the eyes and call instead upon another vision which is to be waked within you, a vision, the birth-right of all, which few turn to use.

9. And this inner vision, what is its operation?

Newly awakened it is all too feeble to bear the ultimate splendour. Therefore the Soul must be trained- to the habit of remarking, first, all noble pursuits, then the works of beauty produced not by the labour of the arts but by the virtue of men known for their goodness: lastly, you must search the souls of those that have shaped these beautiful forms.

But how are you to see into a virtuous soul and know its loveliness?

Withdraw into yourself and look. And if you do not find yourself beautiful yet, act as does the creator of a statue that is to be made beautiful: he cuts away here, he smoothes there, he makes this line lighter, this other purer, until a lovely face has grown upon his work. So do you also: cut away all that is excessive, straighten all that is crooked, bring light to all that is overcast, labour to make all one glow of beauty and never cease chiseling your statue, until there shall shine out on you from it the godlike splendour of virtue, until you shall see the perfect goodness surely established in the stainless shrine.

When you know that you have become this perfect work, when you are self-gathered in the purity of your being, nothing now remaining that can shatter that inner unity, nothing from without clinging to the authentic man, when you find yourself wholly true to your essential nature, wholly that only veritable Light which is not measured by space, not narrowed to any circumscribed form nor again diffused as a thing void of term, but ever immeasurable as something greater than all measure and more than all quantity- when you perceive that you have grown to this, you are now become very vision: now call up all your confidence, strike forward yet a step- you need a guide no longer- strain, and see.

This is the only eye that sees the mighty Beauty. If the eye that adventures the vision be dimmed by vice, impure, or weak, and unable in its cowardly blenching to see the uttermost brightness, then it sees nothing even though another point to what lies plain to sight before it. To any vision must be brought an eye adapted to what is to be seen, and having some likeness to it. Never did eye see the sun unless it had first become sunlike, and never can the soul have vision of the First Beauty unless itself be beautiful.

Therefore, first let each become godlike and each beautiful who cares to see God and Beauty. So, mounting, the Soul will come first to the Intellectual-Principle and survey all the beautiful Ideas in the Supreme and will avow that this is Beauty, that the Ideas are Beauty. For by their efficacy comes all Beauty else, but the offspring and essence of the Intellectual-Being. What is beyond the Intellectual-Principle we affirm to be the nature of Good radiating Beauty before it. So that, treating the Intellectual-Kosmos as one, the first is the Beautiful: if we make distinction there, the Realm of Ideas constitutes the Beauty of the Intellectual Sphere; and The Good, which lies beyond, is the Fountain at once and Principle of Beauty: the Primal Good and the Primal Beauty have the one dwelling-place and, thus, always, Beauty's seat is There.

Plotinus. *Enneads*. 6. 8 and 9; Stephen McKenna translator.

7. If the mind reels before something thus alien to all we know, we must take our stand on the things of this realm and strive thence to see. But, in the looking, beware of throwing outward; this Principle does not lie away somewhere leaving the rest void; to those of power to reach, it is present; to the inapt, absent. In our daily affairs we cannot hold an object in mind if we have given ourselves elsewhere, occupied upon some other matter; that very thing must be before us to be truly the object of observation. So here also; preoccupied by the impress of something else, we are withheld under that pressure from becoming aware of The Unity; a mind gripped and fastened by some definite thing cannot take the print of the very contrary. As Matter, it is agreed, must be void of quality in order to accept the types of the universe, so and much more must the soul be kept formless if there is to be no infixed impediment to prevent it being brimmed and lit by the Primal Principle.

In sum, we must withdraw from all the extern, pointed wholly inwards; no leaning to the outer; the total of things ignored, first in their relation to us and later in the very idea; the self put out of mind in the contemplation of the Supreme; all the commerce so closely There that, if report were possible, one might become to others reporter of that communion.

Such converse, we may suppose, was that of Minos, thence known as the Familiar of Zeus; and in that memory he established the laws which report it, enlarged to that task by his vision There. Some, on the other hand, there will be to disdain such citizen service, choosing to remain in the higher: these will be those that have seen much.

God- we read- is outside of none, present unperceived to all; we break away from Him, or rather from ourselves; what we turn from we cannot reach; astray ourselves, we cannot go in search of another; a child distraught will not recognise its father; to find ourselves is to know our source.

8. Every soul that knows its history is aware, also, that its movement, unthwarted, is not that of an outgoing line; its natural course may be likened to that in which a circle turns not upon some external but on its own centre, the point to which it owes its rise. The soul's movement will be about its source; to this it will hold, poised intent towards that unity to which all souls should move and the divine souls always move, divine in virtue of that movement; for to be a god is to be integral with the Supreme; what stands away is man still multiple, or beast.

Is then this "centre" of our souls the Principle for which we are seeking?

We must look yet further: we must admit a Principle in which all these centres coincide: it will be a centre by analogy with the centre of the circle we know. The soul is not a circle in the sense of the geometric figure but in that it at once contains the Primal Nature [as centre] and is contained by it [as circumference], that it owes its origin to such a centre and still more that the soul, uncontaminated, is a self-contained entity.

In our present state- part of our being weighed down by the body, as one might have the feet under water with all the rest untouched- we bear- ourselves aloft by that- intact part and, in that, hold through our own centre to the centre of all the centres, just as the centres of the great circles of a sphere coincide with that of the sphere to which all belong. Thus we are secure.

If these circles were material and not spiritual, the link with the centres would be local; they would lie round it where it lay at some distant point: since the souls are of the Intellectual, and the Supreme still loftier, we understand that contact is otherwise procured, that is by those powers which connect Intellectual agent with Intellectual Object; this all the more, since the Intellect grasps the Intellectual object by the way of similarity, identity, in the sure link of kindred. Material mass cannot blend into other material mass: unbodied beings are not under this bodily limitation; their separation is solely that of otherness, of differentiation; in the absence of otherness, it is similars mutually present.

Thus the Supreme as containing no otherness is ever present with us; we with it when we put otherness away. It is not that the Supreme reaches out to us seeking our communion: we reach towards the Supreme; it is we that become present. We are always before it: but we do not always look: thus a choir, singing set in due order about the conductor, may turn away from that centre to which all should attend: let it but face aright and it sings with beauty, present effectively. We are ever before the Supreme- cut off is utter dissolution; we can no longer be- but we do not always attend:

when we look, our Term is attained; this is rest; this is the end of singing ill; effectively before Him, we lift a choral song full of God.

9. In this choiring, the soul looks upon the wellspring of Life, wellspring also of Intellect, beginning of Being, fount of Good, root of Soul. It is not that these are poured out from the Supreme lessening it as if it were a thing of mass. At that the emanants would be perishable; but they are eternal; they spring from an eternal principle, which produces them not by its fragmentation but in virtue of its intact identity: therefore they too hold firm; so long as the sun shines, so long there will be light.

We have not been cut away; we are not separate, what though the body-nature has closed about us to press us to itself; we breathe and hold our ground because the Supreme does not give and pass but gives on for ever, so long as it remains what it is.

Our being is the fuller for our turning Thither; this is our prosperity; to hold aloof is loneliness and lessening. Here is the soul's peace, outside of evil, refuge taken in the place clean of wrong; here it has its Act, its true knowing; here it is immune. Here is living, the true; that of to-day, all living apart from Him, is but a shadow, a mimicry. Life in the Supreme is the native activity of Intellect; in virtue of that converse it brings forth gods, brings forth beauty, brings forth righteousness, brings forth all moral good; for of all these the soul is pregnant when it has been filled with God. This state is its first and its final, because from God it comes, its good lies There, and, once turned to God again, it is what it was. Life here, with the things of earth, is a sinking, a defeat, a failing of the wing.

That our good is There is shown by the very love inborn with the soul; hence the constant linking of the Love-God with the Psyches in story and picture; the soul, other than God but sprung of Him, must needs love. So long as it is There, it holds the heavenly love; here its love is the baser; There the soul is Aphrodite of the heavens; here, turned harlot, Aphrodite of the public ways: yet the soul is always an Aphrodite. This is the intention of the myth which tells of Aphrodite's birth and Eros born with her.

The soul in its nature loves God and longs to be at one with Him in the noble love of a daughter for a noble father; but coming to human birth and lured by the courtships of this sphere, she takes up with another love, a mortal, leaves her father and falls.

But one day coming to hate her shame, she puts away the evil of earth, once more seeks the father, and finds her peace.

Those to whom all this experience is strange may understand by way of our earthly longings and the joy we have in winning to what we most desire- remembering always that here what we love is perishable, hurtful, that our loving is of mimicries and turns awry because all was a mistake, our good was not here, this was not what we sought. There only is our veritable love and There we may hold it and be with it, possess it in its verity no longer submerged in alien flesh. Any that have seen know what I have in mind: the soul takes another life as it approaches God; thus restored it feels that the dispenser of true life is There to see, that now we have nothing to look for but, far otherwise, that we must put aside all else and rest in This alone, This become, This alone, all the earthly environment done away, in haste to be free, impatient of any bond holding us to the baser, so that with our being entire we may cling about This, no part in us remaining but through it we have touch with God.

Thus we have all the vision that may be of Him and of ourselves; but it is of a self-wrought to splendour, brimmed with the Intellectual light, become that very light, pure, buoyant, unburdened, raised to Godhood or, better, knowing its Godhood, all aflame then- but crushed out once more if it should take up the discarded burden.

10. But how comes the soul not to keep that ground?

Because it has not yet escaped wholly: but there will be the time of vision unbroken, the self hindered no longer by any hindrance of body. Not that those hindrances beset that in us which has veritably seen; it is the other phase of the soul that suffers and that only when we withdraw from vision and take to knowing by proof, by evidence, by the reasoning processes of the mental habit. Such logic is not to be confounded with that act of ours in the vision; it is not our reason that has seen; it is something greater than reason, reason's Prior, as far above reason as the very object of that thought must be.

In our self-seeing There, the self is seen as belonging to that order, or rather we are merged into that self in us which has the quality of that order. It is a knowing of the self restored to its purity. No doubt we should not speak of seeing; but we cannot help talking in dualities, seen and seer, instead of, boldly, the achievement of unity. In this seeing, we neither hold an object nor trace distinction; there is no two. The man is changed, no longer himself nor self-belonging; he is merged with the Supreme, sunken into it, one with it: centre coincides with centre, for on this higher plane things that touch at all are one; only in separation is there duality; by our holding away, the Supreme is set outside. This is why the vision baffles telling; we cannot detach the Supreme to state it; if we have seen something thus detached we have failed of the Supreme which is to be known only as one with ourselves.

Enneads 6. 9. 7-10; McKenna translator.

13. Gregory of Nyssa and Dionysius the Areopagite Selections

Gregory of Nyssa

Darkness

What does it mean that Moses entered the darkness and then saw God in it? What is now recounted seems somehow to be contradictory to the first theophany, for then the Divine was beheld in light but now he is seen in darkness. Let us not think that this is at variance with the sequence of things we have contemplated spiritually. Scripture teaches by this that religious knowledge comes at first to those who receive it as light. Therefore what is perceived to be contrary to religion is darkness, and the escape from darkness comes about when one participates in light. But as the mind progresses and, through an ever greater and more perfect diligence, comes to apprehend reality, as it approaches more nearly to contemplation, it sees more clearly what of the divine nature is uncontemplated.

For leaving behind everything that is observed, not only what sense comprehends but also what the intelligence thinks it sees, it keeps on penetrating deeper until by the intelligence's yearning for understanding it gains access to the invisible and the incomprehensible, and there it sees God. This is the true knowledge of what is sought; this is the seeing that consists in not seeing, because that which is sought transcends all knowledge, being separated on all sides by incomprehensibility as by a kind of darkness. Wherefore John the sublime, who penetrated into the luminous darkness, says, "No one has ever seen God," thus asserting that knowledge of the divine essence is unattainable not only by men but also by every intelligent creature.

When, therefore, Moses grew in knowledge, he declared that he had seen God in the darkness, that is , that he had then come to know that what is divine is beyond all knowledge and comprehension, for the text says, "Moses approached the dark cloud where God was." What God? He who "made darkness his hiding place," as David says, who also was initiated into the mysteries in the same inner sanctuary.

Once it[the soul] is released from its earthly attachment, it becomes light and swift for its movement upward, souring from below up to the heights.

If nothing comes from above to hinder its upward thrust (for the nature of the Good attracts to itself those who look to it), the soul rises ever higher and will always make its flight yet higher—by its desire of the heavenly things "straining ahead for what is still to come," as the Apostle says.

Made to desire and not to abandon the transcendent height by the things already attained, it makes its way upward without ceasing, ever thought its prior accomplishments renewing its intensity for the flight. Activity directed toward virtue causes its capacity to grow though exertion; this kind of activity alone does not slacken its intensity by the effort, but increases it.

For this reason we also say that the great Moses, as he was becoming ever greater, at no time stopped in his ascent, nor did he set a limit for himself in his upward course. Once having set foot on the ladder which God set up (as Jacob says), he continually climbed to the step above and never ceased to rise higher, because he always found a step higher than the one he had attained.

. . .He shone with glory. And although lifted up through such lofty experiences, he is still unsatisfied in his desire for more. . .

Such an experience seems to me to belong to the soul which loves what is beautiful. Hope always draws the soul from the beauty which is seen to what is beyond, always kindles the desire for the hidden through what is constantly perceived. Therefore, the ardent lover of beauty, although receiving what is always visible as an image of what he desires, yet longs to be filled with every stamp of the archetype.

Dionysius

On the Soul

9. And the soul hath a circular movement viz. an introversion from things without and the unified concentration of its spiritual powers-which gives it a kind of fixed revolution, and, turning it from the multiplicity without, draws it together first into itself, and then (after it has reached this unified condition) unites it to those powers which are a perfect Unity, and thus leads it on unto the Beautiful and Good Which is beyond all things, and is One and is the Same, without beginning or end. And the soul moves with a spiral motion whensoever (according to its capacity) it is enlightened with truths of Divine Knowledge, not in the special unity of its being, but by the process of its discursive reason and by mingled and alternative activities.) And it moves straight forward when it does not enter into itself to feel the stirrings of its spiritual unity (for this, as I said, is the circular motion), but goes forth unto the things around it and feels an influence coming even from the outward world, as from a rich abundance of cunning tokens, drawing it unto the simple unity of contemplative acts.

From *On the Divine Names* 4. 9 by Dionysius the Areopagite published in C.E. Rolt. Translator, *The Divine Names and the Mystical Theology* copyright © 1973 by S.P.C.K. London, 98-99)

On Divine Yearning

Yea, all that exists and that comes into being, exists and comes into being because of the Beautiful and Good; and unto this Object all things gaze and by It are moved' and are conserved, and for the sake of It, because of It and in It, existeth every originating Principle-be this Exemplar, or be it Final or Efficient or Formal or Material Cause-- in a word, all Beginning, all Conservation, and all Ending, or (to sum it up) all things that have being are derived from the Beautiful and Good. Yea, and all things that have no substantial being super-essentially exist in the Beautiful and Good: this is the transcendent Beginning and the transcendent Goal of the universe. For, as Holy Scripture saith: " Of Him, and through Him, and to Him, are all things: to whom be glory for ever. Amen." And hence all things must desire and yearn for and must love the Beautiful and the Good. Yea, and because of It and for Its sake the inferior things yearn for the superior under the mode of attraction, and those of the same rank have a yearning towards their peers under the mode of mutual communion; and the superior have a yearning towards their inferiors under the mode of providential kindness; and each hath a yearning towards itself under the mode of cohesion, and all things are moved by a longing for the Beautiful and Good, to accomplish every outward work and form every act of .will. And true reasoning will also dare to affirm that even the Creator of all things Himself yearneth after all things, createth all things, perfecteth all things, conserveth all things, attracteth all things, through nothing but excess of Goodness. Yea, and the Divine Yearning is naught else than a Good Yearning towards the Good for the mere sake of the Good. For the Yearning which createth all the goodness of the world, being pre-existent abundantly in the Good Creator, allowed Him not to remain unfruitful in Himself, but moved Him to exert the abundance of His powers in the production of the universe. . .

13. And the Divine Yearning brings ecstasy, not allowing them that are touched thereby to belong unto themselves but only to the objects of their affection. This principle is shown by superior things through their providential care for their inferiors, and by those which are co-ordinate through the mutual bond uniting them, and by the inferior through their diviner tendency towards the highest. And hence the great Paul, constrained by the Divine Yearning, and having received a share in its ecstatic power, says, with inspired utterance, " I live, and yet not I but Christ liveth in me": true Sweetheart that he was and (as he says himself) being beside himself unto God, and not possessing his own life but possessing and loving the life of Him for Whom he yearned. And we must dare to affirm (for 'tis the truth) that the Creator of the Universe Himself, in His Beautiful and Good Yearning towards the Universe, is through the excessive yearning of His Goodness, transported outside of Himself in His providential activities towards all things that have being, and is touched by the sweet spell of Goodness, Love and Yearning, and so is drawn from His transcendent throne above all things, to dwell within the heart of all things, through a super-essential and ecstatic power whereby He yet stays within Himself' Hence Doctors call Him " jealous," because He is vehement in His Good Yearning towards the world, and because He stirs men up to a zealous search of yearning desire for Him, and thus shows Himself zealous inasmuch as zeal is always felt concerning things which are desired, and inasmuch as He hath a zeal concerning the creatures for which He careth. In short, both the Yearning and its Object belong to

the Beautiful and the Good, and have therein their pre-existent roots and because of it exist and come into being.

From *On the Divine Names* 4. by Dionysius the Areopagite published in C.E. Rolt. Translator, *The Divine Names and the Mystical Theology* copyright © 1973 by S.P.C.K. London, 100-102, 105-106.

On the Divine Darkness

The Mystical Theology Chapter I What is the Divine Gloom.

Trinity, which exceedeth all Being, Deity, and Goodness!' Thou that instructeth Christians in Thy heavenly wisdom! Guide us to that topmost height of mystic lore- which exceedeth light and more than exceedeth knowledge, where the simple, absolute, and unchangeable mysteries of heavenly Truth lie hidden in the dazzling obscurity of the secret Silence, outshining all brilliance with the intensity of their darkness, and surcharging our blinded intellects with the utterly impalpable and invisible fairness of glories which exceed all beauty! Such be my prayer; and thee, dear Timothy, I counsel that, in the earnest exercise of mystic contemplation, thou leave the senses and the activities of the intellect and all things that the senses or the intellect can perceive, and all things in this world of nothingness, or in that world of being, and that, thine understanding being laid to rest, thou strain (so far as thou mayest) towards an union with Him whom neither being nor understanding can contain. For, by the unceasing and absolute renunciation of thyself and all things, thou shalt in pureness cast all things aside, and be released from all, and so shalt be led upwards to the Ray of that divine Darkness which exceedeth all existence.

These things thou must not disclose to any of the uninitiated, by whom I mean those who cling to the objects of human thought, and imagine there is no super-essential reality beyond; and fancy that they know by human understanding Him that has made Darkness His secret place. And, if the Divine Initiation is beyond such men as these, what can be said of others yet more incapable thereof, who describe the Transcendent Cause of all things by qualities drawn from the lowest order of being, while they deny that it is in any way superior to the various ungodly delusions which they fondly invent in ignorance of this truth? That while it possesses all the positive attributes of the universe (being the universal Cause), yet in a stricter sense It does not possess them, since It transcends them all, wherefore there is no contradiction between affirming and denying that It has them inasmuch as It precedes and surpasses all deprivation, being beyond all positive and negative distinctions ?

Such at least is the teaching of the blessed Bartholomew. For he says that the subject-matter of the Divine Science is vast and yet minute, and that the Gospel combines in itself both width and straitness. Methinks he has shown by these his words how marvelously he has understood that the Good Cause of all things is eloquent yet speaks few words, or rather none; possessing neither speech nor understanding because it exceedeth all things in a super-essential manner, and is revealed in Its naked truth to those alone who pass right through the opposition of fair and foul, and pass beyond the topmost altitudes of the holy ascent and leave behind them all divine enlightenment and voices and heavenly utterances and plunge into the Darkness where truly dwells, as saith the Scripture, that One Which is beyond all things. For not without reason is the blessed Moses bidden first to undergo purification himself and then to separate himself from those who have not undergone it; and after all purification hears the many-voiced trumpets and sees many lights flash forth with pure and diverse-streaming rays, and then stands separate from the multitudes and with the chosen priests presses forward to the topmost pinnacle of the Divine -ascent. Nevertheless he meets not with God Himself, yet he beholds-not Him indeed (for He is invisible) -but the place wherein He dwells. And this I take to signify that the divinest and the highest of the things perceived by the eyes of the body or the mind are but the symbolic language of things subordinate to Him who Himself transcendeth them all. Through these things His incomprehensible presence is shown walking upon those heights of His holy places which are perceived by the mind; and then It breaks forth, even from the things that are beheld and from those that behold them, and plunges the true initiate unto the Darkness of Unknowing wherein he renounces all the apprehensions of his understanding and is enwrapped in that which is wholly intangible and invisible, belonging wholly to Him that is beyond all things and to none else (whether himself or another), and being through the passive stillness of all his reasoning powers united by his highest faculty to Him that is wholly Unknowable, of whom thus by a rejection of all knowledge he possesses a knowledge that exceeds his understanding.

From Chapter 1 *The Mystical Theology* by Dionysius the Areopagite published in C.E. Rolt. Translator, *The Divine Names and the Mystical Theology* copyright © 1973 by S.P.C.K. London, 191-194.

14. Augustine Selections

2. But what was it that delighted me save to love and to be loved? Still I did not keep the moderate way of the love of mind to mind--the bright path of friendship. Instead, the mists of passion steamed up out of the puddly concupiscence of the flesh, and the hot imagination of puberty, and they so obscured and overcast my heart that I was unable to distinguish pure affection from unholy desire. Both boiled confusedly within me, and dragged my unstable youth down over the cliffs of unchaste desires and plunged me into a gulf of infamy. Thy anger had come upon me, and I knew it not. I had been deafened by the clanking of the chains of my mortality, the punishment for my soul's pride, and I wandered farther from thee, and thou didst permit me to do so. I was tossed to and fro, and wasted, and poured out, and I boiled over in my fornications--and yet thou didst hold thy peace, O my tardy Joy! Thou didst still hold thy peace, and I wandered still farther from thee into more and yet more barren fields of sorrow, in proud dejection and restless lassitude.

3. If only there had been someone to regulate my disorder and turn to my profit the fleeting beauties of the things around me, and to fix a bound to their sweetness, so that the tides of my youth might have spent themselves upon the shore of marriage! Then they might have been tranquilized and satisfied with having children, as thy law prescribes, O Lord--O thou who dost form the offspring of our death and art able also with a tender hand to blunt the thorns which were excluded from thy paradise! For thy omnipotence is not far from us even when we are far from thee. Now, on the other hand, I might have given more vigilant heed to the voice from the clouds: "Nevertheless, such shall have trouble in the flesh, but I spare you," and, "It is good for a man not to touch a woman," and, "He that is unmarried cares for the things that belong to the Lord, how he may please the Lord; but he that is married cares for the things that are of the world, how he may please his wife." I should have listened more attentively to these words, and, thus having been "made a eunuch for the Kingdom of Heaven's sake," I would have with greater happiness expected thy embraces.

4. But, fool that I was, I foamed in my wickedness as the sea and, forsaking thee, followed the rushing of my own tide, and burst out of all thy bounds. But I did not escape thy scourges. For what mortal can do so? Thou wast always by me, mercifully angry and flavoring all my unlawful pleasures with bitter discontent, in order that I might seek pleasures free from discontent. But where could I find such pleasure save in thee, O Lord--save in thee, who dost teach us by sorrow, who woundest us to heal us, and dost kill us that we may not die apart from thee. Where was I, and how far was I exiled from the delights of thy house, in that sixteenth year of the age of my flesh, when the madness of lust held full sway in me--that madness which grants indulgence to human shamelessness, even though it is forbidden by thy laws--and I gave myself entirely to it? Meanwhile, my family took no care to save me from ruin by marriage, for their sole care was that I should learn how to make a powerful speech and become a persuasive orator.

From *Confessions* translator Outler, Book 2

7. And I kept seeking for an answer to the question, Whence is evil? And I sought it in an evil way, and I did not see the evil in my very search. I marshaled before the sight of my spirit all creation: all that we see of earth and sea and air and stars and trees and animals; and all that we do not see, the firmament of the sky above and all the angels and all spiritual things, for my imagination arranged these also, as if they were bodies, in this place or that. And I pictured to myself thy creation as one vast mass, composed of various kinds of bodies--some of which were actually bodies, some of those which I imagined spirits were like. I pictured this mass as vast--of course not in its full dimensions, for these I could not know--but as large as I could possibly think, still only finite on every side. But thou, O Lord, I imagined as environing the mass on every side and penetrating it, still infinite in every direction--as if there were a sea everywhere, and everywhere through measureless space nothing but an infinite sea; and it contained within itself some sort of sponge, huge but still finite, so that the sponge would in all its parts be filled from the immeasurable sea.

Thus I conceived thy creation itself to be finite, and filled by thee, the infinite. And I said, "Behold God, and behold what God hath created!" God is good, yea, most mightily and incomparably better than all his works. But yet he who is good has created them good; behold how he encircles and fills them. Where, then, is evil, and whence does it come and how has it crept in? What is its root and what its seed? Has it no being at all? Why, then, do we fear and shun what has no being? Or if we fear it needlessly, then surely that fear is evil by which the heart is unnecessarily stabbed and tortured--and indeed a greater evil since we have nothing real to fear, and yet do fear. Therefore, either that is evil which we fear, or the act of fearing is in itself evil. But, then, whence does it come, since God who is good has made all these things good? Indeed, he is the greatest and chiefest Good, and hath created these lesser goods; but both Creator and created are all good. Whence, then, is evil? Or, again, was there some evil matter out of which he made and formed and ordered it, but left something in his creation that he did not convert into good? But why should this be? Was he powerless to change the whole lump so that no evil would remain in it, if he is the Omnipotent? Finally, why would he make anything at all out of such stuff? Why did he not, rather, annihilate it by his same almighty power? Could evil exist contrary to his will? And if it were from eternity, why did he permit it to be nonexistent for unmeasured intervals of time in the past, and why, then, was he pleased to make something out of it after so long a time? Or, if he wished now all of a sudden to create something, would not an almighty being have chosen to annihilate this evil matter and live by himself--the perfect, true, sovereign, and infinite Good? Or, if it were not good that he who was good should not also be the framer and creator of what was good, then why was that evil matter not removed and brought to nothing, so that he might form good matter, out of which he might then create all things? For he would not be omnipotent if he were not able to create something good without being assisted by that matter which had not been created by himself. Such perplexities I revolved in my wretched breast, overwhelmed with gnawing cares lest I die before I discovered the truth. And still the faith of thy Christ, our Lord and Saviour, as it was taught me by the Catholic Church, stuck fast in my heart. As yet it was unformed on many points and diverged from the rule of right doctrine, but my mind did not utterly lose it, and every day drank in more and more of it.

8. By now I had also repudiated the lying divinations and impious absurdities of the astrologers. Let thy mercies, out of the depth of my soul, confess this to thee also, O my God. For thou, thou only (for who else is it who calls us back from the death of all errors except the Life which does not know how to die and the Wisdom which gives light to minds that need it, although it itself has no need of light--by which the whole universe is governed, even to the fluttering leaves of the trees?)--

thou alone providedst also for my obstinacy with which I struggled against Vindicianus, a sagacious old man, and Nebridius, that remarkably talented young man. The former declared vehemently and the latter frequently--though with some reservation--that no art existed by which we foresee future things. But men's surmises have oftentimes the help of chance, and out of many things which they foretold some came to pass unawares to the predictors, who lighted on the truth by making so many guesses. And thou also providedst a friend for me, who was not a negligent consulter of the astrologers even though he was not thoroughly skilled in the art either--as I said, one who consulted them out of curiosity. He knew a good, deal about it, which, he said, he had heard from his father, and he never realized how far his ideas would help to overthrow my estimation of that art. His name was Firminus and he had received a liberal education and was a cultivated rhetorician. It so happened that he consulted me, as one very dear to him, as to what I thought about some affairs of his in which his worldly hopes had risen, viewed in the light of his so-called horoscope.

Although I had now begun to learn in this matter toward Nebridius' opinion, I did not quite decline to speculate about the matter or to tell him what thoughts still came into my irresolute mind, although I did add that I was almost persuaded now that these were but empty and ridiculous follies. He then told me that his father had been very much interested in such books, and that he had a friend who was as much interested in them as he was himself. They, in combined study and consultation, fanned the flame of their affection for this folly, going so far as to observe the moment when the dumb animals which belonged to their household gave birth to young, and then observed the position of the heavens with regard to them, so as to gather fresh evidence for this so-called art. Moreover, he reported that his father had told him that, at the same time his mother was about to give birth to him [Firminus], a female slave of a friend of his father's was also pregnant. This could not be hidden from her master, who kept records with the most diligent exactness of the birth dates even of his dogs. And so it happened to pass that--under the most careful observations, one for his wife and the other for his servant, with exact calculations of the days, hours, and minutes--both women were delivered at the same moment, so that both were compelled to cast the selfsame horoscope, down to the minute: the one for his son, the other for his young slave. For as soon as the women began to be in labor, they each sent word to the other as to what was happening in their respective houses and had messengers ready to dispatch to one another as soon as they had information of the actual birth--and each, of course, knew instantly the exact time. It turned out, Firminus said, that the messengers from the respective houses met one another at a point equidistant from either house, so that neither of them could discern any difference either in the position of the stars or any other of the most minute points. And yet Firminus, born in a high estate in his parents' house, ran his course through the prosperous paths of this world, was increased in wealth, and elevated to honors. At the same time, the slave, the yoke of his condition being still unrelaxed, continued to serve his masters as Firminus, who knew him, was able to report.

From *Confessions* book 7, Outler Translator

28. Now when deep reflection had drawn up out of the secret depths of my soul all my misery and had heaped it up before the sight of my heart, there arose a mighty storm, accompanied by a mighty rain of tears. That I might give way fully to my tears and lamentations, I stole away from Alypius, for it seemed to me that solitude was more appropriate for the business of weeping. I went far enough away that I could feel that even his presence was no restraint upon me. This was the way I felt at the time, and he realized it. I suppose I had said something before I started up and he noticed that the sound of my voice was choked with weeping. And so he stayed alone, where we had been sitting together, greatly astonished. I flung myself down under a fig tree—how I know not--and gave free course to my tears. The streams of my eyes gushed out an acceptable sacrifice to thee. And, not indeed in these words, but to this effect, I cried to thee: "And thou, O Lord, how long? How long, O Lord? Wilt thou be angry forever? Oh, remember not against us our former iniquities." For I felt that I was still enthralled by them. I sent up these sorrowful cries: "How long, how long? Tomorrow and tomorrow? Why not now? Why not this very hour make an end to my uncleanness?"

29. I was saying these things and weeping in the most bitter contrition of my heart, when suddenly I heard the voice of a boy or a girl I know not which--coming from the neighboring house, chanting over and over again, "Pick it up, read it; pick it up, read it." Immediately I ceased weeping and began most earnestly to think whether it was usual for children in some kind of game to sing such a song, but I could not remember ever having heard the like. So, damming the torrent of my

tears, I got to my feet, for I could not but think that this was a divine command to open the Bible and read the first passage I should light upon. For I had heard how Anthony, accidentally coming into church while the gospel was being read, received the admonition as if what was read had been addressed to him: "Go and sell what you have and give it to the poor, and you shall have treasure in heaven; and come and follow me." By such an oracle he was forthwith converted to thee. So I quickly returned to the bench where Alypius was sitting, for there I had put down the apostle's book when I had left there. I snatched it up, opened it, and in silence read the paragraph on which my eyes first fell: "Not in rioting and drunkenness, not in chambering and wantonness, not in strife and envying, but put on the Lord Jesus Christ, and make no provision for the flesh to fulfill the lusts thereof." I wanted to read no further, nor did I need to. For instantly, as the sentence ended, there was infused in my heart something like the light of full certainty and all the gloom of doubt vanished away.

30. Closing the book, then, and putting my finger or something else for a mark I began--now with a tranquil countenance--to tell it all to Alypius. And he in turn disclosed to me what had been going on in himself, of which I knew nothing. He asked to see what I had read. I showed him, and he looked on even further than I had read. I had not known what followed. But indeed it was this, "Him that is weak in the faith, receive." This he applied to himself, and told me so. By these words of warning he was strengthened, and by exercising his good resolution and purpose--all very much in keeping with his character, in which, in these respects, he was always far different from and better than I--he joined me in full commitment without any restless hesitation.

Then we went in to my mother, and told her what happened, to her great joy. We explained to her how it had occurred--and she leaped for joy triumphant; and she blessed thee, who art "able to do exceedingly abundantly above all that we ask or think." For she saw that thou hadst granted her far more than she had ever asked for in all her pitiful and doleful lamentations. For thou didst so convert me to thee that I sought neither a wife nor any other of this world's hopes, but set my feet on that rule of faith which so many years before thou hadst showed her in her dream about me. And so thou didst turn her grief into gladness more plentiful than she had ventured to desire, and dearer and purer than the desire she used to cherish of having grandchildren of my flesh.

From *Confessions*, book 8 Albert Outler Translator, Collier Books © 1922

15. Cassian and Benedict Selections

John Cassian

Conference 11, Chapter 6   Then the blessed Chaeremon: There are, said he, three things which enable men to control their faults; viz., either the fear of hell or of laws even now imposed; or the hope and desire of the kingdom of heaven; or a liking for goodness itself and the love of virtue. For then we read that the fear of evil loathes contamination: "The fear of the Lord hateth evil." Hope also shuts out the assaults of all faults: for "all who hope in Him shall not fail." Love also fears no destruction from sins, for "love never faileth;"and again: "love covers a multitude of sins." And therefore the blessed Apostle confines the whole sum of salvation in the attainment of those three virtues, saying "Now abideth faith, hope, love, these three." For faith is what makes us shun the stains of sin from fear of future judgment and punishment; hope is what withdraws our mind from present things, and despises all bodily pleasures from its expectation of heavenly rewards; love is what inflames us with keenness of heart for the love of Christ and the fruit of spiritual goodness, and makes us hate with a perfect hatred whatever is opposed to these. And these three things although they all seem to aim at one and the same end(for they incite us to abstain from things unlawful) yet they differ from each other greatly in the degrees of their excellence. For the two former belong properly to those men who in their aim at goodness have not yet acquired the love of virtue, and the third belongs specially to God and to those who have received into themselves the image and likeness of God. For He alone does the things that are good, with no fear and no thanks or reward to stir Him up, but simply from the love of goodness. For, as Solomon says, "The Lord hath made all things for Himself." For under cover of His own goodness He bestows all the fullness of good things on the worthy and the unworthy because He cannot be wearied by wrongs, nor be moved by passions at the sins of men, as He ever remains perfect goodness and unchangeable in His nature.

Chapter 7 If then any one is aiming at perfection, from that first stage of fear which we rightly termed servile (of which it is said: "When ye have done all things say: we are unprofitable servants,") he should by advancing a step mount to the higher path of hope--which is compared not to a slave but to a hireling, because it looks for the payment of its recompense, and as if it were free from care concerning absolution of its sins and fear of punishment, and conscious of its own good works, though it seems to look for the promised reward, yet it cannot attain to that love of a son who, trusting in his father's kindness and liberality, has no doubt that all that the father has is his, to which also that prodigal who together with his father's substance had lost the very name of son, did not venture to aspire, when he said: "I am no more worthy to be called thy son;" for after those husks which the swine ate, satisfaction from which was denied to him, i.e., the disgusting food of sin, as he "came to himself," and was overcome by a salutary fear, he already began to loathe the uncleanness of the swine, and to dread the punishment of gnawing hunger, and as if he had already been made a servant, desires the condition of a hireling and thinks about the remuneration, and says: "How many hired servants of my father have abundance of bread, and I perish here with hunger. I will then return to my father and will say unto him, `Father I have sinned against heaven and before thee, and am no more worthy to be called thy son: make me as one of thy hired servants.'" But those words of humble penitence his father who ran to meet him received with greater affection than that with which they were spoken, and was not content to allow him lesser things, but passing through the two stages without delay restored him to his former dignity of sonship. We also ought forthwith to hasten on that by means of the indissoluble grace of love we may mount to that third stage of sonship, which believes that all that the father has is its own, and so we may be counted worthy to receive the image and likeness of our heavenly Father, and be able to say after the likeness of the true son: "All that the Father hath is mine." Which also the blessed Apostle declares of us, saying: "All things are yours, whether Paul or Apollos or Cephas, or the world, or life, or death, or things present, or things to come; all are yours." And to this likeness the commands of our Saviour also summon us: "Be ye," says He, "perfect, even as your Father in heaven is perfect." For in these persons sometimes the love of goodness is found to be interrupted, when the vigour of the soul is relaxed by some coldness or joy or delight, and so loses either the fear of hell for the time, or the desire of future blessings. And there is indeed in these a stage leading to some advance, which affects us so that when from fear of punishment or from hope of reward we begin to avoid sin we are enabled to pass on to the stage of love, for "fear," says one,"is not in love, but perfect love casteth out fear: for fear hath torment, but he who fears is not perfect in love. We therefore love because God first loved us." We can then only ascend to that true perfection when, as He first loved us for the grace of nothing but our salvation, we also have loved Him for the sake of nothing but His own love alone. Wherefore we must do our best to mount with perfect ardour of mind from this fear to hope, from hope to the love of God, and the love of the virtues themselves, that as we steadily pass on to the love of goodness itself, we may, as far as it is possible for human nature, keep firm hold of what is good.

Chapter 8.   For there is a great difference between one who puts out the fire of sin within him by fear of hell or hope of future reward, and one who from the feeling of divine love has a horror of sin itself and of uncleanness, and keeps hold of the virtue of purity simply from the love and longing for purity, and looks for no reward from a promise for the future, but, delighted with the knowledge of good things present, does everything not from regard to punishment but from delight in virtue. For this condition can neither abuse an opportunity to sin when all human witnesses are absent, nor be corrupted by the secret allurements of thoughts, while, keeping in its very marrow the love of virtue itself, it not only does not admit into the heart anything that is opposed to it, but actually hates it with the utmost horror. For it is one thing for a man in his delight at some present good to hate the stains of sins and of the flesh, and another thing to check unlawful desires by contemplating the future reward; and it is one thing to fear present loss and another to dread future punishment. Lastly it is a much greater thing to be unwilling to forsake good for good's own sake, than it is to withhold consent from evil for fear of evil. For in the former case the good is voluntary, but in the latter it is constrained and as it were violently forced out of a reluctant party either by fear of punishment or by greed of reward. For one who abstains from the allurements of sin owing to fear, will whenever the obstacle of fear is removed, once more return to what he loves and thus will not continually acquire any stability in good, nor will he ever rest free from attacks because he will not secure the sure and lasting peace of chastity. For where there is the disturbance of warfare there cannot help being the danger of wounds. For one who is in the midst of the conflict, even though he is a warrior and by fighting bravely inflicts frequent and deadly wounds on his foes, must still sometimes be pierced by the point of the enemy's sword. But one who has defeated the attack of sins and is now in the enjoyment of the security of peace, and has passed on to the love of virtue itself, will keep this condition of good continually, as he is entirely wrapped up in it, because he believes that nothing can be worse than the loss of his inmost chastity. For he deems nothing dearer or more precious than present purity, to whom a dangerous departure from virtue or a poisonous stain of sin is a grievous punishment. To such an one, I say, neither will regard for the presence of another add anything to his goodness nor will solitude take anything away from it: but as always and everywhere he bears about with him his conscience as a judge not only of his actions but also of his thoughts, he will especially try to please it, as he knows that it cannot be cheated nor deceived, and that he cannot escape it.

Chapter 9.   That love not only makes sons out of servants, but also bestows the image and likeness of God.

And if to anyone relying on the help of God and not on his own efforts, it has been vouchsafed to acquire this state, from the condition of a servant, wherein is fear, and from a mercenary greed of hope, whereby there is sought not so much the good of the donor as the recompense of reward, he will begin to pass on to the adoption of sons, where there is no longer fear, nor greed, but that love which never faileth continually endures. Of which fear and love the Lord in chiding some shows what is befitting for each one: "A son knoweth his own father, and a servant feareth his lord: And if I be a Father, where is My honour: and if I be a Lord, where is my fear?" For one who is a servant must needs fear because "if knowing his lord's will he has done things worthy of stripes, he shall be beaten with many stripes." Whoever then by this love has attained the image and likeness of God, will now delight in goodness for the pleasure of goodness itself, and having somehow a like feeling of patience and gentleness will henceforth be angered by no faults of sinners, but in his compassion and sympathy will rather ask for pardon for their infirmities, and, remembering that for so long he himself was tried by the stings of similar passions till by the Lord's mercy he was saved, will feel that, as he was saved from carnal attacks not by the teaching of his own exertions but by God's protection, not anger but pity ought to be shown to those who go astray; and with full peace of mind will he sing to God the following verse: "Thou hast broken my chains. I will offer to Thee the sacrifice of praise;" and: "except the Lord had helped me, my soul had almost dwelt in hell." And while he continues in this humility of mind he will be able even to fulfil this Evangelic command of perfection: "Love your enemies, do good to them that hate you, and pray for them that persecute you and slander you." And so it will be vouchsafed to us to attain that reward which is subjoined, whereby we shall not only bear the image and likeness of God, but shall even be called sons: "that ye may be," says He "sons of your Father which is in heaven, Who maketh His sun to rise on the good and evil, and sends rain on the just and on the unjust:" and this feeling the blessed John knew that he had attained when he said: "that we may have confidence in the day of judgment, because as He is so are we also in this world." For in what can a weak and fragile human nature be like Him, except in always showing a calm love in its heart towards the good and evil, the just and the unjust, in imitation of God, and by doing good for the love of goodness itself, arriving at that true adoption of the sons of God, of which also the blessed Apostle speaks as follows: "Every one that is born of God doeth not sin, for His seed is in him, and he cannot sin, because he is born of God;" and again: "We know that every one who is born of God sinneth not, but his birth of God preserves him, and the wicked one toucheth him not"? And this must be understood not of all kinds of sins, but only of mortal sins: and if any one will not extricate and cleanse himself from these, for him the aforesaid Apostle tells us in another place that we ought not even to pray, saying: "If a man knows his brother to be sinning a sin not unto death, let him ask, and He will give him life for them that sin not unto death. There is a sin unto death: I do not say that he should ask for it."] But of those which he says are not unto death, from which even those who serve Christ faithfully cannot, with whatever care they keep themselves, be free, of these he says: "If we say that we have no sin we deceive ourselves and the truth is not in us;" and again: "If we say that we have not sinned, we make Him a liar, and His word is not in us." For it is an impossibility for any one of the saints not to fall into those trivial faults which are committed by word, and thought, and ignorance, and forgetfulness, and necessity, and will, and surprise: which though quite different from that sin which is said to be unto death, still cannot be free from fault and blame.

Chapter 10   How it is the perfection of love to pray for one's enemies and by what signs we may recognize a mind that is not yet purified.

When then any one has acquired this love of goodness of which we have been speaking, and the imitation of God, then he will be endowed with the Lord's heart of compassion, and will pray also for his persecutors, saying in like manner: "Father, forgive them, for they know not what they do." But it is a clear sign of a soul that is not yet thoroughly purged from the dregs of sin, not to sorrow with a feeling of pity at the offences of others, but to keep to the rigid censure of the judge: for how will he be able to obtain perfection of heart, who is without that by which, as the Apostle has pointed out, the full requirements of the law can be fulfilled, saying: "Bear one another's burdens and so fulfil the law of Christ," and who has not that virtue of love, which "is not grieved, is not puffed up, thinketh no evil," which "endureth all things, beareth all things." For "a righteous man pitieth the life of his beasts: but the heart of the ungodly is without pity." And so a monk is quite certain to fall into the same sins which he condemns in another with merciless and inhuman severity, for "a stern king will fall into misfortunes," and "one who stops his ears so as not to hear the weak, shall himself cry, and there shall be none to hear him."

Chapter 9.   A question why he has called the feeling of fear and hope imperfect.

Germanus: You have indeed spoken powerfully and grandly of the perfect love of God. But still this fact disturbs us; viz., that while you were exalting it with such praise, you said that the fear of God and the hope of eternal reward were imperfect, though the prophet seems to have thought quite differently about them, where he said: "Fear the Lord, all ye His saints, for they that fear Him lack nothing." And again in the matter of observing God's righteous acts he admits that he has done them from consideration of the reward, saying: "I have inclined my heart to do thy righteous acts forever, for the reward." And the Apostle says: "By faith Moses when he was grown up, denied himself to be the son of Pharaoh's daughter; choosing rather to be afflicted with the people of God than to have the pleasure of sin for a season, esteeming the reproach of Christ greater riches than the treasure of the Egyptians; for he looked unto the reward." How then can we think that they are imperfect, if the blessed David boasted that he did the righteous acts of God in hope of a recompense, and the giver of the Law is said to have looked for a future reward and so to have despised the adoption to royal dignity, and to have preferred the most terrible affliction to the treasures of the Egyptians?

Chapter 12.   Chaeremaon: In accordance with the condition and measure of every mind Holy Scripture summons our free wills to different grades of perfection. For no uniform crown of perfection can be offered to all men, because all have not the same virtue, or purpose, or fervour, and so the Divine Word has in some way appointed different ranks and different measures of perfection itself. And that this is so the variety of beatitudes in the gospel clearly shows. For though they are called blessed, whose is the kingdom of heaven, and blessed are they who shall possess the earth, and blessed are they who shall receive their consolation, and blessed are they who shall be filled, yet we believe that there is a great difference between the habitations of the kingdom of heaven, and the possession of the earth, whatever it be, and also between the reception of consolation and the fullness and satisfaction of righteousness; and that there is a great distinction

between those who shall obtain mercy, and those who shall be deemed worthy to enjoy the most glorious vision of God. "For there is one glory of the sun, and another glory of the moon, and another glory of the stars: for star differeth from star in glory, so also is the resurrection of the dead." While therefore in accordance with this rule holy Scripture praises those who fear God, and says "Blessed are all they that fear the Lord," and promises them for this a full measure of bliss, yet it says again: "There is no fear in love, but perfect love casteth out fear: for fear hath torment. But he that feareth is not yet perfect in love." And again, though it is a grand thing to serve God, and it is said: "Serve the Lord in fear;" and: "It is a great thing for thee to be called My servant;" and: "Blessed is that servant whom his Lord, when He cometh, shall find so doing," yet it is said to the Apostles: "I no longer call you servants, for the servant knoweth not what his Lord doeth: but I call you friends, for all things whatsoever I have heard from my Father, I have made known unto you." And once more: "Ye are My friends, if ye do whatever I command you." You see then that there are different stages of perfection, and that we are called by the Lord from high things to still higher in such a way that he who has become blessed and perfect in the fear of God; going as it is written "from strength to strength," and from one perfection to another, i.e., mounting with keenness of soul from fear to hope, is summoned in the end to that still more blessed stage, which, is love, and he who has been "a faithful and wise servant" will pass to the companionship of friendship and to the adoption of sons. So then our saying also must be understood according to this meaning: not that we say that the consideration of that enduring punishment or of that blessed recompense which is promised to the saints is of no value, but because, though they are useful and introduce those who pursue them to the first beginning of blessedness, yet again love, wherein is already fuller confidence, and a lasting joy, will remove them from servile fear and mercenary hope to the love of God, and carry them on to the adoption of sons, and somehow make them from being perfect still more perfect. For the Saviour says that in His Father's house are "many mansions," and although all the stars seem to be in the sky, yet there is a mighty difference between the brightness of the sun and of the moon, and between that of the morning star and the rest of the stars. And therefore the blessed Apostle prefers it not only above fear and hope but also above all gifts which are counted great and wonderful, and shows the way of love still more excellent than all. For when after finishing his list of spiritual gifts of virtues he wanted to describe its members, he began as follows: "And yet I show unto you a still more excellent way. Though I speak with the tongues of men and angels, and though I have the gift of prophecy and know all mysteries and all knowledge, and though I have all faith so that I can remove mountains, and though I bestow all my goods to feed the poor, and give my body to be burned, but have not love, it profiteth me nothing." You see then that nothing more precious, nothing more perfect, nothing more sublime, and, if I may say so, nothing more enduring can be found than love. For "whether there be prophecies, they shall fail, whether there be tongues, they shall cease, whether there be knowledge, it shall be destroyed," but "love never faileth," and without it not only those most excellent kinds of gifts, but even the glory of martyrdom itself will fail.

Chapter 13.   Of the fear which is the outcome of the greatest love.

Whoever then has been established in this perfect love is sure to mount by a higher stage to that still more sublime fear belonging to love, which is the outcome of no dread of punishment or greed of reward, but of the greatest love; whereby a son fears with earnest affection a most indulgent father, or a brother fears his brother, a friend his friend, or a wife her husband, while there is no dread of his blows or reproaches, but only of a slight injury to his love, and while in every word as well as act there is ever care taken by anxious affection lest the warmth of his love should cool in the very slightest degree towards the object of it. And one of the prophets has finely described the grandeur of this fear, saying: "Wisdom and knowledge are the riches of salvation: the fear of the Lord is his treasure." He could not describe with greater clearness the worth and value of that fear than by saying that the riches of our salvation, which consist in true wisdom and knowledge of God, can only be preserved by the fear of the Lord. To this fear then not sinners but saints are invited by the prophetic word where the Psalmist says: "O fear the Lord, all ye His Saints: for they that fear Him lack nothing." For where a man fears the Lord with this fear it is certain that nothing is lacking to his perfection. For it was clearly of that other penal fear that the Apostle John said that "He who feareth is not made perfect in love, for fear hath punishment." There is then a great difference between this fear, to which nothing is lacking, which is the treasure of wisdom and knowledge, and that imperfect fear which is called "the beginning of wisdom," and which has in it punishment and so is expelled from the hearts of those who are perfect by the incoming of the fullness of love. For "there is no fear in love, but perfect love casteth out fear." And in truth if the beginning of wisdom consists in fear, what will its perfection be except in the love of Christ which, as it contains in it the fear which belongs to perfect love, is called not the beginning but the treasure of wisdom and knowledge?And therefore there is a twofold stage of fear. The one for beginners, i.e., for those who are still subject to the yoke and to servile terror; of which we read: "And the servant shall fear his Lord;" and in the gospel: "I no longer call you servants, for the servant knoweth not what his Lord doeth;" and therefore "the servant," He tells us, "abideth not in the house for ever, but the Son abideth for ever." For He is instructing us to pass on from that penal fear to the fullest freedom of love, and the confidence of the friends and sons of God. Finally the blessed Apostle, who had by the power of the Lord's love already passed through the servile stage of fear, scorns lower things and declares that he has been enriched with good things by the Lord, "for God hath not given us" he says "a spirit of fear but of power and of love and of a sound mind." Those also who are inflamed with a perfect love of their heavenly Father, and whom the Divine adoption has already made sons instead of servants, he addresses in these words: "For ye have not received the spirit of bondage again to fear, but ye received the spirit of adoption, whereby we cry, Abba, Father." It is of this fear too, that the prophet spoke when he would describe that sevenfold spirit, which according to the mystery of the Incarnation, full surely descended on the God man: "And there shall rest upon Him the Spirit of the Lord: the Spirit of wisdom and of understanding, the Spirit of counsel and of might, the Spirit of knowledge and of true godliness," and in the last place he adds as something special these words: "And the Spirit of the fear of the Lord shall fill Him." Where we must in the first place notice carefully that he does not say "and there shall rest upon Him the Spirit of fear," as he said in the earlier cases, but he says "there shall fill Him the Spirit of the fear of the Lord." For such is the greatness of its richness that when once it has seized on a man by its power, it takes possession not of a portion but of his whole mind. And not without good reason. For as it is closely joined to that love which "never faileth," it not only fills the man, but takes a lasting and inseparable and continual possession of him in whom it has begun, and is not lessened by any allurements of temporal joy or delights, as is sometimes the case with that fear which is cast out. This then is the fear belonging to perfection, with which we are told that the God-man, who came not only to redeem mankind, but also to give us a pattern of perfection and example of goodness, was filled. For the true Son of God "who did no sin neither was guile found in His mouth," could not feel that servile fear of punishment.

The Works of John Cassian. Translated with Prolegomena and notes by Rev.. Edgar C. S. Gibson, M.A., From: *A Select Library of Nicene and Post-Nicene Fathers of the Christian Church,* Second Series, Volume 11 New York © 1894, Conference 11

Benedict

Listen carefully, my son, to the master's instructions, and attend to them with the ear of your heart. This is the advice from a father who loves you; welcome it, and faithfully put it into practice. 2 The labor of obedience will bring you back to him from whom you had drifted through the sloth of disobedience. 3 This message of mine is for you, then, if you are ready to give up your own will, once and for all, and armed with the strong and noble weapons of obedience to do battle for the true King, Christ the Lord.

4 First of all, every time you begin a good work, you must pray to him most earnestly to bring it to perfection. 5 In his goodness, he has already counted us as his sons, and therefore we should never grieve him by our evil actions. 6 With his good gifts which are in us, we must obey him at all times that he may never become the angry father who disinherits his sons, 7 nor the dread lord, enraged by our sins, who punishes us forever as worthless servants for refusing to follow him to glory.

8 Let us get up then, at long last, for the Scriptures rouse us when they say: It is high time for us to arise from sleep (Rom 13:11). 9 Let us open our eyes to the light that comes from God, and our ears to the

voice from heaven that every day calls out this charge: 10 If you hear his voice today, do not harden your hearts (Ps 94[95]:8). 11 And again: You that have ears to hear, listen to what the Spirit says to the churches (Rev 2:7). 12 And what does he say? Come and listen to me, sons; I will teach you the fear of the Lord (Ps 33[34]:12). 13 Run while you have the light of life, that the darkness of death may not overtake you (John 12)

Seeking his workman in a multitude of people, the Lord calls out to him and lifts his voice again: 15 Is there anyone here who yearns for life and desires to see good days? (Ps 33[34]:13). 16 If you hear this and your answer is "I do," God then directs these words to you: 17 If you desire true and eternal life, keep your tongue free from vicious talk and your lips from all deceit; turn away from evil and do good; let peace be your quest and aim (Ps 33[34]:14-15). 18 Once you have done this, my eyes will be upon you and my ears will listen for your prayers; and even before you ask me, I will say to you: Here I am (Isa. 58:9).

19 What, dear brothers, is more delightful than this voice of the Lord calling to us? 20 See how the Lord in his love shows us the way of life. 21 Clothed then with faith and the performance of good works, let us set out on this way, with the Gospel for our guide, that we may deserve to see him who has called us to his kingdom (1Thess 2:12).

If we wish to dwell in the tent of this kingdom, we will never arrive unless we run there by doing good deeds. 23 But let us ask the Lord with the Prophet: Who will dwell in your tent, O Lord; who will find rest upon your holy mountain? (Ps 14[15]:1). 24 After this question, brothers, let us listen well to what the Lord says in reply, for he shows us the way to his tent. 25 One who walks without blemish, he says, and is just in all his dealings; 26 who speaks the truth from his heart and has not practiced deceit with his tongue; 27 who has not wronged a fellow man in any way, nor listened to slanders against his neighbor (Ps 14[15]:2-3). 28 He has foiled the evil one, the devil, at every turn, flinging both him and his promptings far from the sight of his heart. While these temptations were still   young, he caught hold of them and dashed them against Christ (Ps 14[15]: 4; 136[137]:9).

29 These people fear the Lord, and do not become elated over their good deeds; they judge it is the Lord's power, not their own, that brings about the good in them. 30 They praise (Ps 14[15]:4) the Lord working in them, and say with the Prophet: Not to us, Lord, not to us give the glory, but to your name alone (Ps 113[115:1]:9). 31 In just this way Paul the Apostle refused to take credit for the power of his preaching.

He declared: By God's grace I am what I am (1 Cor. 15:10). 32 And again he said: He who boasts should make his boast in the Lord (2 Cor 10:17). 33 That is why the Lord says in the Gospel: Whoever hears these words of mine and does them is like a wise man who built his house upon rock; 34 the floods came and the winds blew and beat against the house, but it did not fall: it was founded on rock. (Mt. 7)

With this conclusion, the Lord waits for us daily to translate into action, as we should, his holy teachings. 36 Therefore our life span has been lengthened by way of a truce, that we may amend our misdeeds. 37 As the Apostle says: Do you not know that the patience of God is leading you to repent (Rom 2:4)? 38 And indeed the Lord assures us in his love: I do not wish the death of a sinner, but that he turn back to me and live (Ezek 33:11). 39 Brothers, now that we have asked the Lord who will dwell in his tent, we have heard the instructions for dwelling in it, but only if we fulfill the obligations of those who dwell there. 40 We must, then, prepare our hearts and bodies for the battle of holy obedience to his instructions. 41 What is not possible to us by nature, let us ask the Lord to supply by the help of his grace. 42 If we wish to reach eternal life, even as we avoid the torments of hell, 43 then--while there is still time, while we are in this body and have time to accomplish all these things by the light of life—44 we must run and do now what will profit us forever.

Therefore we intend to establish a school for the Lord's service. 46 In drawing up its regulations, we hope to set down nothing harsh, nothing burdensome. 47 The good of all concerned, however, may prompt us to a little strictness in order to amend faults and to safeguard love. 48 Do not be daunted immediately by fear and run away from the road that leads to salvation. It is bound to be narrow at the outset. 49 But as we progress in this way of life and in faith, we shall run on the path of God's commandments, our hearts overflowing with the inexpressible delight of love. 50 Never swerving from his instructions, then, but faithfully observing his teaching in the monastery until death, we shall through patience share in the sufferings of Christ that we may deserve also to share in his kingdom. Amen.

16. Bernard of Clairvaux Selections

Chapter 8 Of the first degree of love: wherein man loves God for self's sake

Love is one of the four natural affections, which it is needless to name since everyone knows them. And because love is natural, it is only right to love the Author of nature first of all. Hence comes the first and great commandment, 'Thou shalt love the Lord thy God.' But nature is so frail and weak that necessity compels her to love herself first; and this is carnal love, wherewith man loves himself first and selfishly, as it is written, 'That was not first which is spiritual but that which is natural; and afterward that which is spiritual' (I Cor. 15:46). This is not as the precept ordains but as nature directs: 'No man ever yet hated his own flesh' (Eph. 5:29). But if, as is likely, this same love should grow excessive and, refusing to be contained within the restraining banks of necessity, should overflow into the fields of voluptuousness, then a command checks the flood, as if by a dike: 'Thou shalt love thy neighbor as thyself'. And this is right: for he who shares our nature should share our love, itself the fruit of nature. Wherefore if a man find it a burden, I will not say only to relieve his brother's needs, but to minister to his brother's pleasures, let him mortify those same affections in himself, lest he become a transgressor. He may cherish himself as tenderly as he chooses, if only he remembers to show the same indulgence to his neighbor. This is the curb of temperance imposed on thee, O man, by the law of life and conscience, lest thou shouldest follow thine own lusts to destruction, or become enslaved by those passions which are the enemies of thy true welfare. Far better divide thine enjoyments with thy neighbor than with these enemies. And if, after the counsel of the son of Sirach, thou goest not after thy desires but refrainest thyself from thine appetites (Ecclus. 18:30); if according to the apostolic precept having food and raiment thou art therewith content (I Tim. 6:8), then thou wilt find it easy to abstain from fleshly lusts which war against the soul, and to divide with thy neighbors what thou hast refused to thine own desires. That is a temperate and righteous love which practices self-denial in order to minister to a brother's necessity. So our selfish love grows truly social, when it includes our neighbors in its circle.

But if thou art reduced to want by such benevolence, what then? What indeed, except to pray with all confidence unto Him who giveth to all men liberally and upbraideth not (James 1:5), who openeth His hand and filleth all things living with plenteousness (Ps. 145:16). For doubtless He that giveth to most men more than they need will not fail thee as to the necessaries of life, even as He hath promised: 'Seek ye the Kingdom of God, and all those things shall be added unto you' (Luke 12:31). God freely promises all things needful to those who deny themselves for love of their neighbors; and to bear the yoke of modesty and sobriety, rather than to let sin reign in our mortal body (Rom. 6:12), that is indeed to seek the Kingdom of God and to implore His aid against the tyranny of sin. It is surely justice to share our natural gifts with those who share our nature.

But if we are to love our neighbors as we ought, we must have regard to God also: for it is only in God that we can pay that debt of love aright. Now a man cannot love his neighbor in God, except he love God Himself; wherefore we must love God first, in order to love our neighbors in Him. This too, like all good things, is the Lord's doing, that we should love Him, for He hath endowed us with the possibility of love. He who created nature sustains it; nature is so constituted that its Maker is its protector for ever. Without Him nature could not have begun to be; without Him it could not subsist at all. That we might not be ignorant of this, or vainly attribute to ourselves the beneficence of our Creator, God has determined in the depths of His wise counsel that we should be subject to tribulations. So when man's strength fails and God comes to his aid, it is meet and right that man, rescued by God's hand, should glorify Him, as it is written, 'Call upon Me in the time of trouble; so will I hear thee, and thou shalt praise Me' (Ps. 50:15). In such wise man, animal and carnal by nature, and loving only himself, begins to love God by reason of that very self-love; since he learns that in God he can accomplish all things that are good, and that without God he can do nothing.

Chapter IX. Of the second and third degrees of love

So then in the beginning man loves God, not for God's sake, but for his own. It is something for him to know how little he can do by himself and how much by God's help, and in that knowledge to order himself rightly towards God, his sure support. But when tribulations, recurring again and again, constrain him to turn to God for unfailing help, would not even a heart as hard as iron, as cold as marble, be softened by the goodness of such a Savior, so that he would love God not altogether selfishly, but because He is God? Let frequent troubles drive us to frequent supplications; and surely, tasting, we must see how gracious the Lord is (Ps. 34:8). Thereupon His goodness once realized draws us to love Him unselfishly, yet more than our own needs impel us to love Him selfishly: even as the Samaritans told the woman who announced that it was Christ who was at the well: 'Now we believe, not because of thy saying: for we have heard Him ourselves, and know that this is indeed the Christ, the savior of the world' (John 4:42). We likewise bear the same witness to our own fleshly nature, saying, 'No longer do we love God because of our necessity, but because we have tasted and seen how gracious the Lord is'. Our temporal wants have a speech of their own, proclaiming the benefits they have received from God's favor. Once this is recognized it will not be hard to fulfill the commandment touching love to our neighbors; for whosoever loves God aright loves all God's creatures. Such love is pure, and finds no burden in the precept bidding us purify our souls, in obeying the truth through the Spirit unto unfeigned love of the brethren (I Peter 1:22). Loving as he ought, he counts that command only just. Such love is thankworthy, since it is spontaneous; pure, since it is shown not in word nor tongue, but in deed and truth (I John 3:18); just, since it repays what it has received. Whoso loves in this fashion, loves even as he is loved, and seeks no more his own but the things which are Christ's, even as Jesus sought not His own welfare, but ours, or rather ourselves. Such was the psalmist's love when he sang: 'O give thanks unto the Lord, for He is gracious' (Ps. 118:1). Whosoever praises God for His essential goodness, and not merely because of the benefits He has bestowed, does really love God for God's sake, and not selfishly. The psalmist was not speaking of such love when he said: 'So long as thou doest well unto thyself, men will speak good of thee'(Ps. 49:18). The third degree of love, we have now seen, is to love God on His own account, solely because He is God.

Chapter X. Of the fourth degree of love: wherein man does not even love self save for God's sake

How blessed is he who reaches the fourth degree of love, wherein one loves himself only in God! Thy righteousness standeth like the strong mountains, O God. Such love as this is God's hill, in the which it pleaseth Him to dwell. 'Who shall ascend into the hill of the Lord?' 'O that I had wings like a dove; for then would I flee away and be at rest.' 'At Salem is His tabernacle; and His dwelling in Sion.' (Ps.55:6; 76:2; 120:5). When shall this flesh and blood, this earthen vessel which is my soul's tabernacle, attain thereto? When shall my soul, rapt with divine love and altogether self-forgetting, yea, become like a broken vessel, yearn wholly for God, and, joined unto the Lord, be one spirit with Him? When shall she exclaim, 'My flesh and my heart faileth; but God is the strength of my heart and my portion for ever' (Ps. 73:26). I would count him blessed and holy to whom such rapture has been vouchsafed in this mortal life, for even an instant to lose thyself, as if thou wert emptied and lost and swallowed up in God, is no human love; it is celestial. But if sometimes a poor mortal feels that heavenly joy for a rapturous moment, then this wretched life envies his happiness, the malice of daily trifles disturbs him, this body of death weighs him down, the needs of the flesh are imperative, the weakness of corruption fails him, and above all brotherly love calls him back to duty. Alas! that voice summons him to re-enter his own round of existence; and he must ever cry out lamentably, 'O Lord, I am oppressed: undertake for me' (Isa. 38:14); and again, 'O wretched man that I am! who shall deliver me from the body of this death?'(Rom. 7:24).

Seeing that the Scripture saith, God has made all for His own glory (Isa. 43:7), surely His creatures ought to conform themselves, as much as they can, to His will. In Him should all our affections center, so that in all things we should seek only to do His will, not to please ourselves. And real happiness will come, not in gratifying our desires or in gaining transient pleasures, but in accomplishing God's will for us: even as we pray everyday: 'Thy will be done in earth as it is in heaven' (Matt. 6:10). O chaste and holy love! O sweet and gracious affection! O pure and cleansed purpose, thoroughly washed and purged from any admixture of selfishness, and sweetened by contact with the divine will! To reach this state is to become godlike. As a drop of water poured into wine loses itself, and takes the color and savor of wine; or as a bar of iron, heated red-hot, becomes like fire itself, forgetting its own nature; or as the air, radiant with sun-beams, seems not so much to be illuminated as to be light itself; so in the saints all human affections melt away by some unspeakable transmutation into the will of God. For how could God be all in all, if anything merely human remained in man? The substance will endure, but in another beauty, a higher power, a greater glory. When will that be? Who will see, who possess it? 'When shall I come to appear before the presence of God?' (Ps. 42:2). 'My heart hath talked of Thee, Seek ye My face: Thy face, Lord, will I seek' (Ps. 27:8). Lord, thinkest Thou that I, even I shall see Thy holy temple?

In this life, I think, we cannot fully and perfectly obey that precept, 'Thou shalt love the Lord thy God with all thy heart, and with all thy soul, and with all thy strength, and with all thy mind'(Luke 10:27). For here the heart must take thought for the body; and the soul must energize the flesh; and the strength must guard itself from impairment. And by God's favor, must seek to increase. It is therefore impossible to offer up all our being to God, to yearn altogether for His face, so long as we must accommodate our purposes and aspirations to these fragile, sickly bodies of ours. Wherefore the soul may hope to possess the fourth degree of love, or rather to be possessed by it, only when it has been clothed upon with that spiritual and immortal body, which will be perfect, peaceful, lovely, and in everything wholly subjected to the spirit. And to this degree no human effort can attain: it is in God's power to give it to whom He wills. Then the soul will easily reach that highest stage, because no lusts of the flesh will retard its eager entrance into the joy of its Lord, and no troubles will disturb its peace. May we not think that the holy martyrs enjoyed this grace, in some degree at least, before they laid down their victorious bodies? Surely that was immeasurable strength of love which enraptured their souls, enabling them to laugh at fleshly torments and to yield their lives gladly. But even though the frightful pain could not destroy their peace of mind, it must have impaired somewhat its perfection.

From *On Loving God*, electronic version by Adam Worger: Http://www.bible.net /books/oo24/index.htm

17. Bonaventure Selections

Prologue

1. In the beginning the First Principle, from whom all other illuminations descend as from the Father of lights, by whom is every best gift and every perfect gift, that is the Eternal Father, I do invoke through His Son, Our Lord Jesus Christ, with the intercession of the Most Holy Virgin Mary, the same Mother of Our God and Lord Jesus Christ, and of blessed Francis, our leader and father, to grant that the eyes of our mind (be) illumined to direct our feet in the way of His peace, which exceeds every sense; which peace Our Lord Jesus Christ has proclaimed and has given; the renewer of whose preaching was our Father Francis, announcing at the beginning and end of all his preaching peace, in every salutation choosing peace, in every contemplation longing towards ecstatic peace, as a citizen of that Jerusalem, concerning which that man of peace speaks, who with those who hate peace, was peaceable: Ask for those things which are for the peace of Jerusalem. For he knew, that the throne of Solomon was not but in peace, since it was written: In peace is made His place, and His dwelling in Sion.

2. When therefore by the example of most blessed Father Francis I sought with a panting spirit this peace, I a sinner, who, unworthy in all things ascend to the place of the most blessed father himself as seventh in the Minister generalship after his transitus; it happened that with the divine permission about the (time of) the Transitus of the Blessed himself, in the thirty-third year (of its celebration, 1259 A.D.), I turned aside with the love of seeking peace of spirit towards mount Alverna as towards a quiet place, and staying there, while I considered in mind some mental ascensions into God, among others there occurred that miracle, which in the aforesaid place happened to blessed Francis himself, that is, of the vision of the Seraph winged after the likeness of the Crucified. In consideration of which it suddenly seemed to me, that that vision showed the suspension of our father himself in

contemplating Him and the way, through which one arrives at that (suspension).

3. For through those six wings there can be rightly understood six suspensions of illumination, by which the soul as if to certain steps or journeys is disposed, to pass over to peace through ecstatic excesses of Christian wisdom. The way is, however, naught but through the most ardent love of the Crucified, who to this extent transformed Paul rapt to the third heaven into Christ, that he said: to Christ I have been crucified, now not I; but Christ lives in me; who also to this extent absorbed the mind of Francis, since the mind lay in the flesh, while he bore about the most sacred stigmata of the Passion in his own flesh for two years before his death. The likenesses of the six seraphic wings intimates six stair-like illuminations, which begin from creatures and lead through even to God, to Whom no one rightly enters except through the Crucified. For he who does not enter through the gate, but ascends by another way, that one is a thief and mercenary. If anyone indeed goes inside through the gate, he will step in and out and find pasture. On which account John says in the Apocalypse: Blessed are they who wash their vestments in the Blood of the Lamb, to have power in the Tree of life, and to step in the city through the gates; as if he said, that through contemplation one cannot step into the supernal Jerusalem, unless he enter through the Blood of the Lamb as through a gate. For one has not been disposed in any manner to divine contemplations, which lead towards mental excesses except with Daniel one be a man of desires. Moreover desires are inflamed in us in a two-fold manner, that is through the clamour of praying, which makes one shout from a groan of the heart, and though the lightning of speculation, by which the mind thoroughly turns itself most directly and most intensely towards the rays of light.

4. Therefore to the groan of praying through Christ crucified, through whose Blood we are purged from the filth of vice, I indeed first invite the reader, lest perhaps he believes that reading without unction, speculation without devotion, investigation without admiration, circumspection without exultation, industry without piety, knowledge without charity, understanding without humility, study apart from divine grace, gaze apart from divinely inspired wisdom is sufficient for him. Anticipated, therefore, by divine grace, for the humble and pious, the compunct and devout, for those anointed with the oil of gladness both for the lovers of divine wisdom and for those inflamed with desire for it, I propose the following speculations to be free for those willing

to magnify, admire and even take a taste of God, intimating, that too little or nothing is the proposed, exterior gaze, unless the mirror of our mind has been wiped and polished. Exert yourself, therefore, man of God, before the sting of conscience bites again, and before you raise your eyes towards the rays of wisdom glittering in His reflections, lest by chance from the sight itself of the rays you fall into the more grave pit of shadows.

5. Moreover it is pleasing to divide the tract into seven chapters, by previewing their titles for an easier understanding of the things to be said. I ask therefore, that the intention of the one writing be thought of more, than the work, more the sense of the things said than the uncultured speech, more its truth than its charm, more the exercise of affection than the erudition of the intellect. Because as it is, one must not run perfunctorily through the course of these speculations, but ruminate (on them) with the greatest of lingering.

Here ends the Prologue of Bonaventure's *The Journey of the Mind into God.*

Reprinted with permisiion of the Franciscan Archive, translated from the Quarrachi Edition of the Opera Omnia S. Bonaventurae, http://www.ccel.org/b/bonaventure/journey/journey.html

18. John Ruusbroec and Julian of Norwich Selections

Ruusbroec

Chapter 65 Of Three Kinds of Most Inward Practices

This most inward life is practised in three ways. At times, the inward man performs his introspection simply, according to the fruitive tendency, above all activity and above all virtues, through a simple inward gazing in the fruition of love. And here he meets God without intermediary. And from out the Divine Unity, there shines into him a simple light and this light shows him Darkness and Nakedness and Nothingness. In the Darkness, he is enwrapped and falls into somewhat which is in no wise, even as one who has lost his way. In the Nakedness, he loses the perception and discernment of all things, and is transfigured and penetrated by a simple light. In the Nothingness, all his activity fails him, for he is vanquished by the working of God's abysmal love, and in the fruitive inclination of his spirit he vanquishes God, and becomes one spirit with him. And in this oneness with the Spirit of God, he enters into a fruitive tasting and possesses the Being of God. And he is filled, according to the measure in which he has sunk himself in his essential being with the abysmal delights and riches of God. And from these riches an envelopment and a plenitude of sensible love flow forth into the unity of the higher powers. And from this plenitude of sensible love, a savoury and penetrating satisfaction flows forth into the heart and the bodily powers. And through this inflow the man becomes immovable within, and helpless as regards himself and all his works. And in the deeps of his ground he knows and feels nothing, in soul or in body, but a singular radiance with a sensible well-being and an all-pervading saviour. This is the first way, and it is the way of emptiness; for it makes a man empty of all things, and lifts him up above activity and above all the virtues. And it unites the man with

God, and brings about a firm perseverance in the most interior practices which he can cultivate. When, however, any restlessness, or working of the virtues, puts intermediaries, or images, between the inward man and the naked introversion which he desires, then he is hindered in this exercise; for this way consists in a going out, beyond all things, into the Emptiness. This is the first form of the most inward exercise.

At times such an inward man turns towards God with ardent desire and activity; that he may glorify and honour Him, and offer up and annihilate in the love of God, his selfhood and all that he is able to do. And here he meets God through an intermediary. This intermediary is the gift of Savouring Wisdom, the ground and origin of all virtues; which enkindles and moves all good men according to the measure of their love, and at times so greatly stirs and enkindles the inward man through love, that all the gifts of God, and all that God may give, except the gift of Himself, seem too little to him, and cannot satisfy him, but rather increase his impatience. For he has an inward perception or feeling in his ground; where all the virtues begin and end, where love dwells, and where with ardent desire he offers up all his virtues to God. And here the hunger and thirst of love become so great that he perpetually surrenders himself, and gives up his own works, and empties himself, and is noughted in love, for he is hungry and thirsty for the taste of God; and, at each irradiation of God, he is seized by God, and more than ever before is newly touched by love. Living he dies, and dying he lives again. And in this way the desirous hunger and thirst of love are renewed in him every hour.

This is the second way, which is the way of longing, in which love dwells in the Divine likeness, and longs and craves to unite itself with God. This way is more profitable and honourable to us than the first, for it is the source of the first; for none can enter into the rest which is above all works save the man who has loved love with desire and with activity. And this is why the grace of God and our active love must both go before and follow after; that is to say, they must be practised both before and after. For without acts of love we cannot merit anything, neither achieve God, nor keep the possession of that which we have acquired through the works of love. And for this reason no one who has power over himself, and can practise love, should be idle. When, however, a good man lingers in any gift of God, or any creature, he will be hindered in this most inward exercise; for this exercise is a hunger which nothing can still, save God alone.

From these two ways the third way arises; and this is an inward life according to justice. Now understand this: God comes to us without ceasing both with means and without means, and demands of us both action and fruition, in such a way that the one never impedes, but always strengthens, the other. And therefore the most inward man lives his life in these two ways: namely, in work and in rest. And in each he is whole and undivided; for he is wholly in God because he rests in fruition, and he is wholly in himself because he loves in activity· and he is perpetually called and urged by God to renew both the rest and the work. And the justice of the spirit desires to pay every hour that which is demanded of it by God. And therefore, at each irradiation of God, the spirit turns inward, in action and in fruition; and thus it is renewed in every virtue, and is more deeply immersed in fruitive rest. For God gives, in one gift, Himself and His gifts; and the spirit gives, at each introversion, itself and all its works. For by means of the simple irradiation of God and the fruitive tendency and melting away of love, the spirit has been united with God, and is incessantly transported into rest. And through the gifts of Understanding and Savouring Wisdom, it is touched in an active way, and perpetually enlightened and enkindled in love. And there is shown and presented to it in the spirit all that one may desire. It is hungry and thirsty, for it beholds the food of the angels and the heavenly drink. It works diligently in love, for it beholds its rest. It is a pilgrim; and it sees its country In love it strives for victory; for it sees its crown. Consolation, peace, joy, beauty and riches, and all that can delight it, are shown without measure in ghostly images to the reason which is enlightened in God. And through this showing and the touch of God, love remains active. For this just man has established a true life in the spirit, in rest and in work, which shall endure eternally; but, after this life, it shall be changed into a higher state. Thus the man is just; and he goes towards God with fervent love in eternal activity; and he goes in God with fruitive inclination in eternal rest. And he dwells in God, and yet goes forth towards all creatures in universal love, in virtue, and in justice. And this is the supreme summit of the inward life. All those men who do not possess both rest and work in one and the same exercise, have not yet attained this justice. This just man cannot be hindered in his introversion, for he turns inward both in fruition and in work; but he is like to a double mirror, which receives images on both sides. For in his higher part, the man receives God with all His gifts; and, in his lower part, he receives bodily images through the senses. Now he can enter into himself at will, and can practise justice without hindrance. But man is unstable in this life, and that is why he often turns outwards, and works in the senses, without need and without the command of the enlightened reason; and thus he falls into venial sins. But in the loving introversion of the just man all venial sins are like to drops of water in a glowing furnace.

And with this I leave the inward life.

From John Ruusbroeck *The Adornment of the Spiritual Marriage,* translated from the Flemish by C. A. Wynschenk, edited with an introduction and notes by E. Underhill. http://www.ccel.org/r/ruysbroeck/adornment/adornment1.0.txt

Julian of Norwich

CHAPTER LIX

"Jesus Christ that doeth Good against evil is our Very Mother: we have our Being of Him where the Ground of Motherhood beginneth, -- with all the sweet Keeping by Love, that endlessly followeth." And all this bliss we have by Mercy and Grace: which manner of bliss we might never have had nor known but if that property of Goodness which is God had been contraried: whereby we have this bliss. For wickedness hath been suffered to rise contrary to the Goodness, and the Goodness of Mercy and Grace contraried against the wickedness and turned all to goodness and to worship, to all these that shall be saved. For it is the property in God which doeth good against evil. Thus Jesus Christ that doeth good against evil is our Very Mother: we have our Being of Him, -- where the Ground of Motherhood beginneth, -- with all the sweet keeping of Love that endlessly followeth. As verily as God is our Father, so verily God is our Mother; and that shewed He in all, and especially in these sweet words where He saith: I it am. That is to say, I it am, the Might and the Goodness of the Fatherhood; I it am, the Wisdom of the Motherhood; I it am, the Light and the Grace that is all blessed Love: I it am, the Trinity, I it am, the Unity· I am the sovereign Goodness of all manner of things. I am that maketh thee to love: I am that maketh thee to long: I it am, the endless fulfilling of all true desires.

From Julian of Norwich. *Shewings*, edited by Grace Warrack, Metheun & Co. London, 1901, p. 147 http://www.ccel.org/j/julian/revelations/revelations.html

NOTES

[1] See Robin Scroggs. *Paul for a New Day* (Philadelphia: Fortress, 1977), p.32, n. 8; see LXX version of Isa.1:23 and 2 Sm 13:1.

[2] For a well documented treatment of this see A. Heschel. *The Prophets.*

[3] See S. Lilla *Clement of Alexandria*(N.Y.: Oxford University Press, 1971), pp.14-59, esp. 35-36.

[4] See Lilla pp.201-208.

[5] See R.A.Markus *Augustine: A Collection of Critical Essays* (Garden City, N.Y. :1972), pp. 27-28.

[6] I say "appears" because this theory of forms contains considerable controversy. See R. O'Connell. *Plato* (Fordham University Press, 1997), pp. 76 ff. and David Gallop *Phaedo* (Oxford: Clarendon Press, 1975), pp.93 ff. for good discussions.

[7] See J.M. Rist *Plotinus* (Cambridge University Press, 1967), pp. 66 ff. for discussion of freedom and necessity in Plotinian emanation.

[8] See Etienne Gilson, "Regio dissisimilitudinis de Platon a Saint Bernard of Clairvaux," *Medieval Studies* 9:108-130. For Key texts see Plato *Statesman* 273d; *Theatetus* 176 a, b; Plotinus *Enneads* 1.8.10; Augustine *Confessions* 7; Bernard of Clairvaux *On Grace and Free Will* 10:32; *Sermons on the Song of Songs* 36.5; *Letters* 81.2; William of St. Thierry *Commentary on the Canticle of Canticles* 1.65.

[9] For other light imagery see *Enneads* 6. 3. .9; 5. 1. 1; 5. 1. 6.; 5. 3.12. Plato also uses light imagery as well as Augustine' in his *Confessions* 4. 15. 25; 7.10. 16.

[10] See *Gregory of Nyssa.*, vol. V of A Select Library of Nicene and Post-Nicene Fathers (N.Y.: Christian Literature Company, 1893) chapter 1, p.3 "The Life and Writings of Gregory of Nyssa" for a discussion of Gregory's purported marriage as well as for an English version of *On Virginity.*

[11] His friend Gregory Nazianzen is one of the first to employ this language that is so often associated with the later Dionysius. See A. H. Armstrong. *The Cambridge History of Later Greek and Early Medieval Philosophy*(Cambridge University Press, 1967), pp. 444-446; some of the inspiration to link knowledge with purification may well come from Plato *Phaedo* 66 and 67 where he speaks of the importance of purification from bodily distractions. In Christian literature see Clement of Alexandria *Stromata* 7. 3: "the humble heart with right knowledge is the holocaust of God; each man who is admitted to holiness being illuminated in order to indissoluble union."

[12] B. McGinn. *Christian Spirituality I*(Crossroads, 1985), p.133.

[13] See for examples Thomas Hand. *Saint Augustine on Prayer* (Newman Press, 1963).

[14] This teaching on slave, hireling, offspring via Basil has been incorporated

into the *Catechism of the Catholic Church*: "The practice of the moral life animated by charity gives to the Christian the spiritual freedom of the children of God. He no longer stands before God as a slave, in servile fear, or as a mercenary looking for wages, but as a son responding to the love of him who 'first loved us': [1 Jn. 4:19] If we turn away from evil out of fear of punishment, we are in the position of slaves. If we pursue the enticement of wages, . we resemble mercenaries. Finally if we obey for the sake of the good itself and out of love for him who commands we are in the position of children." [St. Basil, Reg. fus. tract., prol. 3: PG 31, 896 B.; *Catechism of the Catholic Church* # 1828).]

[15] See De Vogue, *Community and Abbot in the Rule of St. Benedict* (Cistercian Publications,1988), pp.394ff.

[16] See Julian of Norwich *Showings* (Paulist Press, 1978), p. 23.

BIBLIOGRAPHY

A. H. Armstrong. *The Cambridge History of Later Greek and Early Medieval Philosophy.* Cambridge University Press, 1967.
_____. *Plotinus.* London: Allen and Unwin, 1953.
_____. *Plotinus.* Cambridge: Harvard University Press, 1967.
Augustine. *The Trinity.* Translated by Stephen McKenna. Washington: Catholic University, 1967
_____. *Confessions.* Translated by Albert Outler. N.Y. Collier Books, 1922.
_____. *Confessions of St. Augustine.* Translated by E.B.Pusey. N.Y.: Airmont Publishing, 1969.
_____. *Confessons of St. Augustine.* Translated by Rex Warner. N.Y.: New American Library, 1963.
Benedict. *St. Benedict's Rule for Monasteries.*Liturgical Press,1948.
Bernard of Clairvaux. *On Grace and Free Choice.* Kalamazoo: Cistercian Publications, 1977.
_____. *The Steps of Humility.* Cambridge MA: Harvard University Press, 1950.
_____ *Treatises II.* Washington: Cistercian Publications, 1974.
_____. *On the Love of God.* Newman Press, 1951.
Bonaventure. Translated by Ewert Cousins. N.Y.: Paulist 1978.
_____. *The Works of Bonventure.* Translated by Jose De Vinjk Chicago: Franciscan Herald Press, 1973
Bouyer, Louis. *The Spirituality of the New Testament and the Fathers.* N.Y.: Seabury, 1963.
Bynum, Caroline. "The Cistercian Conception of Community"*Harvard Theological Review.* Vol. 68(1975):273-286.
Casey, M. "The Journey from Fear to Love: John Cassian's Road Map" in Pauline Allen, et. al. *Prayer and Spirituality*, published by Center for Early Christian Studies, Australian Catholic University, 1998.
Cassian, John. *The Conferences.* N.Y.: Paulist Press, 1997.
Clement D'Alexandrie. *Les Stromates.* Translated by Marcel Caster. Paris: Editions de Cerf, 1951
_____. *Miscellanies Book VII.* Edited by John Fenton, Anthony Hort, and Joseph Mayor. NY: Macmillan, 1902.
_____. *Christ the Educator.* Translated by Simon P. Wood. N.Y.: Fathers of the Church, 1954.

Cousins, Ewert. *Bonaventure and the Coincidence of Opposites.*Chicago:Franciscan Herald Press, 1977.

De Vogue.A. *Community and Abbot in the Rule of St. Benedict.* Kalamazoo: Cistercian Publications, 1988.

Dionysius the Areopagite *The Divine Names and The Mystical Theology.* Translated by C.E.Rolt. London SPCK 1975.

Timothy Fry, Timothy. *RB 1980:The Rule of St. Benedict.* Liturgical Press, 1981.

Gallop, David. *Phaedo.* Oxford: Clarendon Press, 1975.

Gilson, Etienne. *The Christian Philosophy of Saint Augustine.* N.Y.: Vintage Books, 1967.

Gregory of Nyssa. *The Life of Moses.* N.Y.: Paulist Press, 1978.

Julian of Norwich. *Showings.* N.Y.: Paulist Press, 1978)

Kirchemeyer, Jean. "Grecque"(Eglise) in *Dictionnaire de Spiritualite,* Vol. VII. Paris: Beauchesne, 1971.

Lamarche, Paul. "Image et Resemblance" in *Dictionnaire de Spiritualite,* Vol. VII. Paris Beauchesne, 1971.

Lilla, Salvatore. *Clement of Alexandria.* NY: Oxford U. Press, 1971.

Lossky, Vladimir. *The Mystical Theology of the Eastern Church.* Crestwood, NY:St. Vladimir's Seminary Press, 1976.

Markus, R.A. *Augustine.* N.Y. Doubleday , 1972.

McGinn, Bernard. *Christian Spirituality I.* Crossroads, 1985.

_____. *The Foundations of Mysticism. Vol. I.* Crossroad, 1992.

Molinari, Paul. Julian of Norwich: *The Teaching of a 14th Century Mystic.* London: Longmans, Green and Co., 1958.

O'Connell, Robert. *Plato* N.Y.: Fordham University Press, 1997.

Plato. *The Collected Dialogues of Plato.* N.Y. Pantheon Books, 1966.

_____. *The Dialogues of Plato.* Translated by B. Jowett. NY: Scribner, 1873.

Plotinus. *The Six Enneads.* translated by Stephen MacKenna and B.S. Page.Chicago: Encyclopaedia Britannica, 1952.

Pieper, Josef. *About Love.* Chicago, Franciscan Herald, 1974.

Rist, J.M. *Plotinus: The Road to Reality.* Cambridge:Cambridge University Press, 1967.

Ruusbroec, John. *The Spiritual Espousals and Other Works* N.Y.: Paulist Press, 1985.

Philip Schaff and Henry Wace. *Gregory of Nyssa: Dogmatic Treatises,* Vol. V of A Select Library of Nicene and Post-Nicene Fathers of the Christian Church. Christian Literature Company, 1893.